soma

Celebrating 35 Years of
Penguin Random House India

ADVANCE PRAISE FOR THE BOOK

'The Soma poems, which had occupied A.K. Ramanujan through the 1970s up to the early 1980s, are here seen for the first time . . . To have left them interred in boxes in a library would have meant, among other things, losing a critical moment of our literary history'—A.K. Mehrotra, poet, literary critic and translator

'Thrilling, provocative and intellectually stimulating, Soma takes us on a detour through A.K. Ramanujan's archive, to illuminate a pivotal yet long-eclipsed moment in his trajectory. It contextualizes Ramanujan in the aftermath of the 1960s counterculture, with its openness to doors of perception, whether scriptural or hallucinogenic. With sensitivity and erudition, Guillermo Rodríguez and Krishna Ramanujan reconstruct this "missing period" in the life of the remarkable author of *The Striders* and *Second Sight*, the pioneering translator of Kannada vacanas and Tamil Sangam poems: a fertile period of luminous vision and ecstatic articulation during which his diverse preoccupations with poetry and translation, mythology and anthropology, popular culture and science came together in a blaze of intensity. This volume—with its elegant montage of previously unpublished poems, newly commissioned essays and thoughtful annotation—generates a new and inspiring approach to seeing and situating the work of a seminal poet and scholar'—Ranjit Hoskote, poet, translator and cultural theorist

'This fascinating book leads us into the alchemical heat of a poet's workshop. The result is an absorbing read not just for Ramanujan aficionados, but for those interested in poems—their shadowy origins, and the crackling synapses that go into their making. Here is A.K. Ramanujan hyperlinked: poet, scholar, man, translator of the Virashaiva poets of Karnataka and the Tamil mystics, Nammalvar and Manikkavachakar. Through a mosaic of unpublished drafts and fragments, this book explores the middle phase in the literary life of one of modern India's most distinguished poet–translators'—Arundhathi Subramaniam, poet

soma

Poems by
A.K. RAMANUJAN

Edited by
Guillermo Rodríguez
and Krishna Ramanujan

PENGUIN
VIKING

An imprint of Penguin Random House

VIKING

USA | Canada | UK | Ireland | Australia
New Zealand | India | South Africa | China | Singapore

Viking is part of the Penguin Random House group of companies
whose addresses can be found at global.penguinrandomhouse.com

Published by Penguin Random House India Pvt. Ltd
4th Floor, Capital Tower 1, MG Road,
Gurugram 122 002, Haryana, India

First published in Viking by Penguin Random House India 2023

10 9 8 7 6 5 4 3 2 1

The views and opinions expressed in this book are the editors' own and the
facts are as reported by them which have been verified to the extent possible,
and the publishers are not in any way liable for the same.

ISBN 9780670098040

Typeset in Monticello LT Pro by Manipal Technologies Limited, Manipal
Printed at Thomson Press India Ltd, New Delhi

www.penguin.co.in

Contents

Editors' Note and Acknowledgements

The A.K. Ramanujan Papers at the University of Chicago contain numerous diaries and journals, a careful selection of which was edited by us and published as *Journeys: A Poet's Diary* (2019). The papers also comprise innumerable drafts of poems by A.K. Ramanujan (AKR) that were either published during his lifetime in three poetry collections (1966, 1971 and 1986) or brought out in posthumous collections (1995 and 2001). What stands out in the discarded poetry drafts is an intriguing series of poems titled *Soma*, which the poet–scholar intended to publish as a new collection around 1982 that never saw the light of day. A handful of these unpublished poems were first documented in Guillermo Rodríguez's *When Mirrors Are Windows: A View of A.K. Ramanujan's Poetics* (2016), and a few more appeared in *Journeys: A Poet's Diary* alongside the diary entries. *Journeys* was an attempt to trace AKR's life journey—in his own voice—as a writer and poet, and him maturing into a remarkable intellectual luminary. The diaries introduced the reader to his complex creative personality, since we hear the writer at work observing the particulars of life as he tackles the larger issues of human relations and artistic inspiration.

In several ways, *Soma: Poems by A.K. Ramanujan* is a companion volume to *Journeys*. It opens another door to the poet's atelier during a crucial period in his life, the 1970s to the early 1980s, filling a gap between the publication of his poetry collections *Relations* (1971) and *Second Sight* (1986). These years were filled with episodes of personal turmoil, yet they proved to be full of creativity for Ramanujan as a poet and especially as a translator; *Speaking of Siva*, a collection of medieval Kannada bhakti poems from the Vīraśaiva tradition, was published in 1973, and his translations of the Tamil Ālvār poetry, *Hymns for the Drowning: Poems for Visnu by Nammālvār*, came out in 1981.

This edited volume on the theme of Soma includes twenty-two 'Soma poems' by A.K. Ramanujan, which serve as the book's centrepiece. Within the author's personal files, several manuscripts titled 'Soma' exist, and as he worked on this collection in the 1970s and early 1980s and continued adding poetic material, many of its poems were eventually discarded. Some were included in Ramanujan's third book of original poetry, which he finally chose to title *Second Sight* (1986) and contained essentially a new body of work in form and scope. In the 'Soma' folders and earlier related poetry files, we found a series of unpublished drafts whose style, theme and tone set them apart from his earlier work; the verse seemed more autobiographical and experimental, perhaps freed of constraint, both poetic and cultural.

Though some of these 'Soma poems' have been published (albeit in different versions) in recent years, they are shown here collectively for the first time. They exist as a re-construction of a theme-inspired work of art that remained unpublished as such during the poet's lifetime and was so far only known in fragments. Some of the compositions were still working drafts, as they appear in the (mostly typed) manuscripts that he continued to revisit through the years, but we have taken great care to include the latest versions and revisions in this collective volume. Most of these poems, however, were 'finished' pieces. For several reasons that will be described in this book, they were never published while Ramanujan was alive, with the exception of the last two, which he chose to include in *Second Sight*. It is our hope that readers will appreciate and savour these fresh-sounding, unrestrained poems, seeing them collected here for the first time as a body of work. Through them, readers will gain access to a particular period in Ramanujan's literary history, projecting yet another portrait of the multi-layered poet, with the translator and scholar in the background.

For Ramanujan, who infused his diverse, 'promiscuous' knowledge into his poetry, the various concepts of Soma and its uses extend to creativity, translation, metaphysics and Vedic religious history. Thus the 'Soma poems' are like the hub of a wheel on which this volume turns, with the essays and an interview serving as spokes that provide context to the multifarious concept of Soma. The supplementary material is intended to surround these unique, unadorned—yet beautiful—poems with literary, aesthetic, scientific and historical perspectives on Soma and their relationships to Ramanujan's poetry.

Beneath these poems lies the weight of a rich and ancient history of the Vedic religion, the Rig Veda and a mysterious psychoactive—possibly hallucinogenic—plant that Vedic priests pressed to make an ambrosia that they drank during sacrificial rituals, a drink that potentially turbocharged their mystical experiences. For the last two and a half centuries, scholars have made exhaustive attempts at identifying the Soma plant. At its core, the search for Soma is also a quest for the meaning of consciousness and to understand forces that may have shaped Hindu culture and the genesis of early religions, as one line of argument suggests that nascent religion itself co-evolved with mind-altering plants.

Our effort to contextualize the poems begins with two essays: the opening piece, 'Hummel's Miracle: The Search for Soma', provides a brief overview of the importance of the Soma drink for Vedic priests, outlines a quest for the plant's identity from the late 1960s to the present, and explores how this history is tied to the Soma poems themselves. Whereas 'The "Ordinary Mystery" Trip: Soma in A.K. Ramanujan's Poetry' takes a deep dive into Ramanujan's layered and inclusive perspective on Soma and the original process that feeds into his poetics during a specific period of his career as a translator–poet.

The additional features that add historical context and substance to this volume include the essay 'The Post-Vedic History of the Soma Plant' by Wendy Doniger, originally published in 1968 in the landmark book by R. Gordon Wasson titled *Soma: Divine Mushroom of Immortality,* which influenced Ramanujan's and many other scholars' and writers' perceptions of Soma. Doniger's essay surveys the history of scholarly attempts to identify the Soma plant from the late eighteenth century until 1968. It has never been reprinted, and comes here with a delightful preface specially written by Doniger for this volume. And as a final addition, the book contains a newly edited version of an interview conducted in Chicago in 1982 in which the Malayali poet K. Ayyappa Paniker converses with Ramanujan on poetry writing, multilingualism, translation and the latter's new poetry collection, which was then to be titled *Soma*. The interview offers the reader a peek into A.K. Ramanujan's creative mindset in the early 1980s, when this set of poems was particularly relevant for him.

In conclusion, while this book focuses on the 'Soma poems' and the artistic process of an Indian writer living and writing in America, it also intends to raise other questions concerning the scholarly, literary and cultural contexts of a fascinating period in Western Indology and its cultural history when many Eastern (Indian) philosophies and traditions were debated, absorbed and transformed. Some of these became so popular that they influence our understanding of contemporary culture to this day.

We are very grateful to A.K. Mehrotra for writing the foreword, which provides a glimpse of the depth and perceptiveness of his critical scholarship on contemporary Indian poetry. His short prose piece resonates with the exquisitely elegant style of one of the finest living Indian poets writing in English.

Some of the scholars and writers who contributed to this creative dialogue and shared their wisdom and friendship with Ramanujan and with us are no more: K. Ayyappa Paniker, the wise professor and celebrated poet in Malayalam with that ever-present smile and beard, left us in 2006. And the shadow of Girish Karnad, who has been our companion on many other Ramanujan adventures and generously wrote the foreword to *Journeys*, looms large on the canvas of this book. His contours have left a larger void than we are yet to fathom. We would like this volume to be a posthumous token of gratitude and friendship for him.

We also wish to extend a special and heartfelt thank you to Wendy Doniger, whose graciousness and vast knowledge are infused—formally and informally— throughout this volume. She was a long-time colleague and a dear old friend of A.K. Ramanujan.

We are indebted to the Special Collections Research Center at the University of Chicago Library for their ongoing assistance and generosity with this project, and to the team at Penguin Random House India: Meru Gokhale for her unrelenting support for this project; Premanka Goswami for encouraging its publication from the earliest stage; and Karthik Venkatesh, whose sound judgement has kept our efforts on track.

Guillermo Rodríguez and Krishna Ramanujan

Foreword

Arvind Krishna Mehrotra

A.K. Ramanujan died suddenly at sixty-four, much work still ahead of him. A lot of it had been published while he was alive but plenty remained in various stages of completion in his papers, and of the *Collected Essays* (1999), he had made an outline. Since then, 'as if long deep / burial had made them hasty / / for birth and season', several posthumous volumes have appeared, including *Journeys: A Poet's Diary* (2019) and, now, *Soma*. He was his own best archivist and we, his readers, are the beneficiaries.

In 1986, when *Second Sight* came out, Arun Kolatkar jotted down a few lines and deposited the note in an envelope where he kept his undated thoughts. We had been talking about Ramanujan's new book, which is how I am able to date the note. It was discovered after Kolatkar's death and was published, along with several other writings, in an appendix to his *Collected Poems in English* (2010). The note, unusual because Kolatkar seldom expressed an opinion on poets, in public or private, reads:

> Will the real Ramanujan please stand up
> there are several of them as you know
>
> A.K. Ramanujan is a legion rather than an individual
>
> There is a multitude of Ramanujans
> the poet of course, the translator, the folklorist
>
> There are any number of A.K. Ramanujans
> I am personally acquainted/familiar with at least 3 of
>   them
> and love 'em all
>
> I don't claim to know all of them
>
> I wonder whether the Real Ramanujan expresses
>   himself
> through his translations (rather than through his
>   poems)
>
> Ramanujan and his doubles

A parallel discovery has been Ramanujan's allusion, in 'When Soma is abroad', written in 1979, to Kolatkar's *Jejuri* (1977):

> When Soma is abroad
> dialect and jargon glow.

Mother-tongues wear classics on their sleeves,
father tongues loosen,
schoolbook rules run into love and war,
metres breathe, a mountain breeze
or lion cubs
around a majestic father-theme.

Soma, blow again on the coals of Ezekiel's lips,
make chariots of war pirouette among arrows,
bring medicine men in Delhi offices the red robes of
  shamans,
dawn again on the stones of Jejuri
and circle the squares of Konarak.

This is the only time when Ramanujan, in a poem, names his contemporaries either directly (Nissim Ezekiel) or by implication (Arun Kolatkar, Jayanta Mahapatra).[1] The prayer to Soma is for them—the verbs 'blow', 'make', 'bring', 'dawn' and 'circle' at the beginning of each line emphasize this—as much as it is for himself. May the substance or spirit that is being invoked continue to transform those who have once known its disruptive, rule-defying presence.

In 'Men, Women, and Saints', where, in one of the many meanings it has for him, 'Soma . . . is psychedelic, mind-blowing, not exactly social—probably a sacred mushroom.' Ramanujan gives the example of the Vīraśaiva poet–saints of the sixth and seventh centuries of the Common Era who, unlike the Buddha, 'do not appear alone, they seem to appear in droves, in interacting groups of three or four in these early times'. In Ezekiel,

Mahapatra, Ramanujan and Kolatkar, born within seven years of each other, we have a similar 'drove' of poets in what were for Indian poetry in English 'early times'.

Poets tend to squirrel away everything they write. Whatever passes through their inquisitive minds is of interest to them. A poem that has been put aside could have a line or an image that is usable later. They can themselves be surprised by what they almost threw away. Sometimes all that is needed is a change of title to transform a poem permanently. 'Death and the Good Citizen' will remain a poem from *Second Sight*, though its birth name was 'Soma: he thinks of leaving his body (to a hospital)'.

Whether the drafts, fragments and rejected pieces— those that did not quite make it into print while the poet was alive—are of interest to anyone is a different matter. Is it better to leave unused material alone, to be looked at forensically, later if at all? Basil Bunting thought so. Asked by R.B. Woodings, Faber's editorial director, to endorse his mentor Ezra Pound's *Collected Early Poems*, he wrote: 'No doubt it is fitting that maggots consume us in the end, or at least the rubbish we scatter as we go; but I'd rather leave the lid on my dustbin and the earth on my friend's graves . . . Piety takes curious forms: the toenail clippings of Saint What's His Name are revered. I don't think religion is much advanced by that.'

What is on offer here in this book? Are we being fobbed off with the toenail clippings of Saint Ramanujan? Or are we being offered a window into A.K. Ramanujan's workshop where you can hear the clang of metal, the noise of cutting wheels, the intense heat of the furnace, and see the heap of poems that appear discarded but are actually finished? Among them is a poem that has the head of an original poem and the body of a translation, a composite beast such as you come across in Mughal miniatures, which might be a useful way of looking at Ramanujan's work as a whole. The head and the body are so fused that you can only tell them apart because one is in roman, the other in italics, and there is a tail-like footnote. Paradoxically, unlike those in miniature painting, Ramanujan's composite beast is single-specied:

Soma, I said, is no Visnu

Soma, I said, is no Visnu
But Visnu can play Soma,
enter the nests of flesh
to make them sing:

Poets,
 beware, your life is in danger:

the lord of gardens is a thief,
a cheat,
master of illusions;

he came to me,
 a wizard with words,
 sneaked into my body,
my breath,

with bystanders looking on
 but seeing nothing,

he consumed me
life and limb,

and filled me,
made me over
into himself

The footnote tells us that the first four lines are Ramanujan's and the rest of the poem is Nammālvār's, taken from Ramanujan's *Hymns for the Drowning* (1981).

Quotations had been part of Ramanujan's repertoire from the beginning. He embeds a phrase, 'eye-deep', from Ezra Pound's 'Hugh Selwyn Mauberley', in the title poem of his first book, *The Striders* (1966), named for the New England water insect: 'This bug sits / on a landslide of lights / and drowns eye- / deep / into its tiny strip / of sky.' The phrase resurfaces in 'Chicago Zen': 'and you drown, eyes open, / / towards the Indies, the antipodes'. Similarly, in 'On discovering that Soma is a mushroom', he slips in a probing, libidinous line from John Donne:

[I] stand in Soma, warm perishing body
in a cold silver river, the water
is a lover's hand,
in, on, below, between . . .

The hand will remain warm to the last:

License my roving hands, and let them go
Before, behind, between, above, below.
(John Donne, 'To His Mistress Going to Bed')

As often in Ramanujan, one thing flows into another. 'On discovering that Soma is a mushroom' is from 1979, and if you turn to the entry for 24 November 1979 in *Journeys* you find: 'In the last few months I've been teaching with D[avid] Grene Shakespeare's sonnets and Donne's poems. I first read them in college, knew some by heart. I seem to understand them now as I didn't then.'

Soma is the breath of poetry. It loosens the father tongues, Sanskrit and English, and gives the mother tongues, Tamil and Kannada, the easy, formidable heft of the classics, some of which Ramanujan then translated into a father tongue. A tenth-century mystical poet like Nammālvār gets a twentieth-century makeover just as much as English, through translation, gains a new expressive tool. The act of translation is turned into a shamanistic ritual or performance in which the lines have bloodshot eyes and their movement, if you notice the streaky line breaks, is frenzied.

For poets, the state of being in Soma is to be in a state of ecstasy when the dull familiarity that encrusts the commonplace melts away to reveal the 'hard gemlike flame' (the phrase is Walter Pater's) that the most ordinary things possess. Ramanujan's 'things' have possessed this quality from the beginning. 'A Poem of Particulars' is from *The Striders*, its last poem:

> In our city markets
> I have often seen a wicker basket
>   sit
>   upon its single, ample
>   hip,
>   its rattan pattern filled

with another
subtler
bubble-bed pattern of oranges:

pellmell piled
not one with a stain,
some thick-painted green all over,
others
with just a finger-print
of green . . .

'[I]t is only the roughness of the eye,' Pater goes on to say in *The Renaissance* (1873), 'that makes any two persons, things, situations, seem alike'. Ramanujan particularizes ecstatically, as though intoxicated, making each municipal orange, along with the wicker basket holding them, sing. Hence the prayer to Soma—'Soma, blow again . . .' and hence, in *Journeys*, the diary entry of 16 June 1993, 'To write continuously like a trickle stream of thick honey from a slanted bottle.' But hence, too, the warning '*[B]eware, your life is in danger.*' The warning is made both playfully and in earnest. Poet–saints, take Kabir and Tukaram for example, have often been suspected of being crazy, sometimes by their immediate families. One of the poems in *Hymns for the Drowning* is titled 'God's Idiots'. The idiots live precariously and make the lives of those around them precarious as well.

When someone like Ramanujan translates, it is often his own poem he's composing by other means. Through another's he chances upon his voice, and the two had become intertwined. Dyed in a singular colour, you cannot tell them apart. 'In 1968', he writes in *Journeys*:

I finished translating a group of iconoclastic poems from the tenth to the twelfth century called vacanas. I'd begun reading them when I was sixteen and they fitted my own inchoate impulses against caste, the patriarchal oppression of women (especially my mother and sisters), the great division of rich and poor, and even the learned and the illiterate. The following poem was a centrepiece:

The rich
will make temples for Siva.
What shall I,
a poor man,
do?

My legs are pillars,
the body the shrine,
the head
a cupola of gold.

Listen, O lord of the meeting rivers,
things standing shall fall,
but the moving ever shall stay.

(Basavanna 820)

The Basavanna poem could well be the centrepiece of Ramanujan's entire work and also of the way he worked. 'He functioned best,' Molly Daniels–Ramanujan tells us, 'with multiple projects, texts, disciplines, languages, connections, and deadlines.' He could do with little sleep, was restless and was constantly 'moving', even, it appears, in death. She describes the moment: '[H]is body was ice-cold, longer, leaner, and very still. His energy was concentrated on his brow as he chased a thought in flight.'[2]

In a 1982 interview with Ayyappa Paniker, Ramanujan spoke of his 'new book of poems in English', which he was going to call *Soma*. The Soma poems, which had occupied him through the 1970s up to the early 1980s, are here seen for the first time, or, if met with before in whole or part in *Second Sight*, *Hymns for the Drowning* or *Journeys*, are seen in the context they were originally meant to be seen in. To have left them interred in boxes in a library would have meant, among other things, losing a critical moment of our literary history.

ESSAYS

Hummel's Miracle:
The Search for Soma

Krishna Ramanujan

I

In August of 1971, in the afterglow of the psychedelic sixties, my father, the poet–scholar A.K. Ramanujan, swallowed a capsule of the hallucinogen mescaline. As he told me, perhaps some fifteen years later, he had found two capsules in his coat pocket, which a friend had given him. In his telling, he made the whole episode sound casual, claiming he had pocketed the pills and forgotten about them. He said he discovered them that day and popped one on a kind of whim. Then he fell asleep. When he awoke, still lying down, the evening sunlight shone on his arm, and the hairs were golden. 'I was the man with the golden arm,' he told me. Over the next twenty-four hours, he recorded his experience in fragmented, confused and overwhelmingly sensorial verse. By the end of this episode, his writing, like tributaries flowing into a

3

river, had found a main channel, and he began composing lines that led to a series of poems on the theme of Soma,[1] which he explored for the next decade.

I wouldn't say my father was interested in the recreational use of drugs, but he was drawn to experimentation, for the sake of ideas and poetry. He lived with a kind of conflict (one of many) between his Brahminic roots and the desire to be a modern man of the world. By the time he first left India in 1959, he was extremely well-read in western thought and poetry.

The mescaline episode came on the heels of the 1960s, when interest in psychedelics and associated freedoms were particularly relevant.[2] It was also in 1968 that mycologist R. Gordon Wasson published his book, *Soma: Divine Mushroom of Immortality*.[3] Wasson's theory—that Soma was a psychedelic mushroom (not technically a plant)—made a big splash and was widely discussed and debated. We know my father had read Wasson's book, or at the very least he was aware of the argument, because he refers to the mushroom theory in an essay[4] and in his Soma poems.[5]

Soma is at once a god, a plant and an exhilarating and euphoric drink made by pressing the plant's juices, which priests drank for sacrificial rituals. It is also central to the Vedic religion. Of the 1028 hymns of the Rig Veda, 114[6] are dedicated to Soma; an entire Mandala[7] is devoted to it. Soma is also the subject of a great mystery, as the Rig Veda never identifies the species used to make the drink.

Wasson proposed that a mushroom called fly agaric, *Amanita muscaria*,[8] was used to make the Soma drink. He also argued, with interpretations of the Rig Veda, that Soma was specifically hallucinogenic, though the description was later tweaked as 'entheogenic' to clarify its use as a psychoactive substance for religious or spiritual purposes. Though the Soma plant's identity had been extensively investigated for centuries, Wasson's thesis was perhaps the most comprehensive argument up to that time. The book included an essay by Wendy Doniger (Wendy Doniger O'Flaherty, at the time)[9] that was the first to catalogue the prior two-century history (from 1784 to 1967) of attempts by linguists, mythologists and Indologists, anthropologists, historians and ethnobotanists to identify Soma. Doniger's thorough accounting presents 140 theories in chronology on the identity of Soma.[10]

Of its many meanings, Soma is called the Lord of Speech, 'a generator of hymns, a leader of poets, a seer among priests'.[11] The Vedas mention the *kavis*, poets who composed hymns under the spell of Vak, the Goddess of Speech.[12] The drink inspires poets; it 'procreates' thought. Soma is in opposition to alcohol (*sura*), as the *Sathapatha Brahmana* states, 'Soma is truth, prosperity, light; and *sura* untruth, misery, darkness.'[13] It is believed that priests composed hymns of the Rig Veda after drinking Soma;[14] the ability to create a hymn under the influence was one criterion that scholars used for identifying the Soma plant: its effects must leave the poet with enough lucidity to compose.

Along with my father's interest in Aldous Huxley's *Doors of Perception*, and the British writer's hallucinogenic experiences, which were tape recorded with a doctor present,[15] I cannot doubt that AKR's mescaline notes were influenced by what he regarded as Soma, serving as a kind of experiment to achieve poetic inspiration *via* a mind-altering hallucinogen. In this way, perhaps, his effort at imitating the composing practices of Vedic priests was a moment when a dichotomy between his Brahmin roots and his pull to experience a modern and western world came together.

II

The priests who composed the Rig Veda rejoiced in Soma's limitless effects; they call the ambrosia 'the sweet drink of life'; it 'inspires good thoughts and joyous expansiveness to the extreme, that all the gods and mortals seek it together, calling it honey'.[16] The priests who composed the hymns praise how Soma offers entry into a spirit world: 'We have drunk the Soma; we have become immortal; we have gone to the light; we have found the gods.'[17]

The psychedelic potion granted its drinker great power, communion with gods, and even immortality. For these reasons, priests may have been intentionally vague about naming the plant so that they could sequester its extraordinary powers within their domain, protect their sacrificial rituals, and restrict access to the plant among lower castes.

Many scholars believe that the Vedic people moved from the Himalayan mountains to the plains of the Ganges in the second century BCE, and when they did, they no longer had access to the Soma plant. It is also possible that climatic changes or overuse pushed the plant into extinction. The plant of the Rig Veda is the original Soma, generally thought to be one species, while the subsequent *Brahmanas* (commentaries on the Vedas) refer to substitutes and focus on Soma ritual and symbolism.[18] The distinction between the original

Soma and its many surrogates has confused the search for its identity. Moreover, the Rig Veda was composed as a collection of hymns (poems) full of metaphor; the resulting challenges of interpretation can obfuscate and introduce bias.

Wasson's elaborate argument in 1968 that Soma was a hallucinogenic mushroom quickly became the most famous and most often cited Soma theory and was a turning point in the search for the Soma plant's identity. His theory was fresh, a departure from previous candidates, and it was comprehensive and impassioned, infusing renewed vigour into the debate. As Doniger pointed out, while Wasson makes a very strong case for Soma being a hallucinogen, he does not prove that Soma was fly agaric.[19]

Wasson argued that the identification of Soma as fly agaric held up to scrutiny when weighed against the scant clues provided in the Rig Veda. The sacred text never mentions roots, leaves, blossoms or seeds associated with Soma, which is consistent with the mushroom theory.[20] References in the Rig Veda speak of Soma growing at high altitudes: Mujavant,[21] Saryanavat and Arjika[22] are all mountains mentioned as sources of the plant. Wasson pointed out that *A. muscaria* grows in mycorrhizal symbiosis with conifer and birch trees, which are found at heights of 8,000 to 16,000 feet in India.[23]

On another note, Wasson cites a passage in the Mahabharata that refers to an outcast's urine, which when drunk acts as Soma and grants *amrta* (immortality).[24] There is also a line in the Rig Veda that mentions priests peeing Soma but not drinking urine.[25] These clues were important to Wasson, as his previous research had revealed a Siberian custom of drinking the urine of someone who has eaten fly agaric, whereby the body acts as a filter to pass on the mushroom's inebriating qualities, possibly without side effects.[26]

However, many scholars doubted Wasson's mushroom theory. Critics pointed out that the preparation of Soma described in the Rig Veda requires ritualistic pressing to extract juices, which a mushroom does not need. Another doubt was raised, as Brahmins do not eat mushrooms, though no one knows when this practice began.[27] Particularly damning, the intoxicating qualities of fly agaric are extremely variable; Wasson's (and his colleagues') own attempts to recreate an entheogenic experience from fly agaric proved disappointing and never ecstatic.[28] Ethnobotanist Terence McKenna described his own experiments with *A. muscaria* as producing nausea, salivation, blurred vision and stomach cramps, falling far short of the 'rapturous visionary ecstasy that inspired the Vedas'.[29]

Wasson, who by the time of his death in 1986 began to doubt his *A. muscaria* theory, and Terence McKenna suggested that the psilocybin-rich *Stropharia cubensis*, a mushroom that grows in cow dung, might instead be Soma.[30] One main issue with this theory is that, at the time it was proposed, there wasn't clear evidence that it grew in India, especially in the mountains. There is now anecdotal evidence of it in Odisha, but it is also very possible that spores have been introduced more recently.

Another argument that gained traction after 1968 came from David Flattery and Martin Schwartz, who argued that Soma's identity could not be found in the vague, poetic and metaphorical references in the Rig Veda and searched instead for clues about Haoma in the Avesta.[31]

They made a highly detailed case in 1989 for Syrian rue (*Peganum harmala*) as Haoma/Soma. Pharmacologically, Syrian rue contains compounds that act as monoamine-oxidase (MAO) inhibitors, which alone are not especially psychedelic unless administered in high doses, whereby they become toxic.[32] Though Syrian rue has a long history as a medicine, aphrodisiac and intoxicant and was first proposed as Soma by the Indo–Europeanist and philologist Sir William Jones when western discussion of the plant's identity first began in 1794,[33] its effects are described as dream-inducing and lend to passive introversion, unlike the energizing payoff of Soma.[34]

One theory, which many academics accepted, was that Soma was ephedra, whose active ingredient, ephedrine, acts as a mild stimulant. Though the proposal was not new, in 1989, the Indologist Harry Falk published a paper citing many passages in the Rig Veda that describe Soma as a stimulant that kept its users (including the god Indra) awake at night. It gave Indra strength in battle to slay the demonic serpent Vritra.[35] Falk claimed ephedra's effects promoted the alertness required to compose poems. There is a long history, extending back to the fifth century BCE in China, of therapeutic uses of ephedra, and Falk and others point out that Parsis (Zoroastrians) in India carry out modern Hoama ceremonies using ephedra, though people who have observed these rituals claim Parsis do not become intoxicated during such ceremonies.[36] By no means do the effects of ephedra qualify as hallucinogenic. Still, some argued that Soma cannot be divorced from ritual; one always came with the other, and the rituals themselves included fasting, chanting and breathing, which could alter consciousness in themselves and could

Krishna Ramanujan

become downright hallucinatory when combined with ephedrine.[37]

As one might expect, scholars debated the theory that ephedra was Soma. For example, ephedra is common, with fourteen species known in India and new ones being discovered;[38] yet Soma is described in the Rig Veda as rare. Botanist Harri Nyberg claimed that one species, *Ephedra equistina*, grows mainly in the mountains and contains the highest concentration of ephedrine.[39] Some questioned whether ephedra's colour matches the reddish-yellow or golden description of the Soma juice in the Rig Veda.[40] Also, Vedic priests drank Soma during rituals three times a day, and rituals could last many days in a row. While researchers have documented sustained use of entheogens, such as in ayahuasca rituals in the New World, the steady drinking of an ephedra-derived drink, a sharp-tasting stimulant, becomes unpleasant and rattles nerves, like drinking too much coffee, and doesn't live up to descriptions of the rapture, ecstasy and bliss of drinking honey-like Soma.[41]

In 2000, microbiologist and mycologist David Spess made a detailed argument that the water lily (genus *Nymphaea*) and the lotus (genus *Nelumbo*)[42] could be Soma plants. Botanist Andrew McDonald continued this theory, claiming the eastern lotus (*Nelumbo nucifera*) produces a variety of psychoactive compounds, though he adds that the plant's chemical profile requires additional analysis.[43] A comprehensive breakdown of chemicals in the plant's embryo, stamen, flower, leaf and seed has revealed a bevy of beneficial constituents, including antioxidants, anti-steroids, antipyretics, antivirals, and anti-inflammatory qualities, with claims for use in treating diabetes, erectile dysfunction, atherosclerosis, antiaging and more. Yet nowhere in this analysis is there any mention of psychoactive or entheogenic qualities.[44] I could not find convincing evidence that two purported psychoactive compounds, aporphine and nuciferine, found, for example, in the blue lotus (*Nymphae caerulea*) flower, produce entheogenic effects.

Matthew Clark's 2017 proposal that the entheogenic drink is an ayahuasca-like concoction using multiple plants is another more recent suggestion. Two plants mostly used to prepare the entheogen ayahuasca in South America are the *Banisteriopsis caapi* vine and the leaves of *Psychotria viridis*. The latter plant contains the chemical N-N dimethyl-tryptamine (DMT), which is benign unless consumed with a MAO inhibitor, found in *B. caapi*, but in tandem they produce a powerful psychoactive experience, and this works for any two plants containing an MAO inhibitor and DMT.[45] Worldwide, more than sixty plants are known to contain DMT and around seventy contain an MAO inhibitor,[46] with numerous examples growing in South Asia.[47] While interesting, and an idea that opens new doors to investigating mind-altering plants, the theory is almost purely botanical and pharmacological, without enough links to the sacred texts.

III

In the 1970s, a Greek–Russian archaeologist, Viktor Sariandi, while excavating in eastern Turkmenistan, made a discovery that he believed revealed the identity of plants used to make the Soma drink.[48] The excavations at Goňur Depe, the Zoroastrian capital[49] of what was then

called Margiana, unearthed monumental temples[50] dating
to 1900–1500 BCE. In one of the settlements, in a private
room thought to be a hidden inner sanctum for priests,
there was a ceramic bowl containing traces of cannabis and
ephedra. At another settlement, Sariandi and colleagues
found ceramic pots and strainers that might have been used
to separate juice from solid plant matter; they also found a
basin with 'a large quantity'[51] of cannabis. And in a third
settlement, the archaeologists found vessels containing
sediments of ephedra and *Papaver somniferum* (the
poppy plant, from which opium is derived). The vessels
were dug into low brick platforms in the white rooms of
the priests' inner sanctum. Both the Zoroastrian *Avesta*
and the Rig Veda, Mandala IX, contain descriptions of
Soma prepared using tools that Sariandi claimed to have
discovered at Margiana, including vats (for 'soaking the
alkaloid plants'), pressing stones, mortars and pestles.[52]

Evidence of an entheogenic drink dates back to the
Indo–Iranians, whose ancestral lands lay in Central Asia.
Though there are theories about the succession of these
people, one version supports the idea that this culture
splintered around 4000 years ago into two separate
groups. One group flowered into ancient Iranian peoples,
while the other group, the Indo–Aryans, migrated south-
east to present-day Afghanistan and the Indus Valley.
Long before their oral traditions were eventually written
down, the Indo–Aryans composed orally and memorized
the Rig Veda, the text of the pre-Brahminic Vedic religion
(composed between 1700 and 1500 BCE)[53] and the Iranian
group created the *Avesta*, the sacred text of Zoroastrians
(composed around 600 to 400 BCE).[54] Both traditions
revolved around a plant-based, spiritually enhancing

drink. The Zoroastrians called this sacred drink Hoama
and the Vedic people refer to it as Soma. In this way,
Sariandi's find might relate to a common ancestor of Soma
and Hoama. 'The excavations documentally [*sic*] proved
that poppy, cannabis and ephedra were used for making
the soma-haoma drinks, and thickets of these plants were
found in excess in the vicinity of the excavated temples of
Margiana,' Sariandi claimed.[55]

One might think such an archaeological discovery
would, at the very least, tilt a centuries-old debate
to identify the Soma plant(s). The findings certainly
qualified for achieving 'Hummel's miracle',[56] a reference
to German pharmacologist and botanist Karl Hummel,
who wrote that unless a miracle occurs in the form of an
archaeological find that contains a Soma plant sample, the
question of 'what is Soma' will remain a topic of debate.[57]

As was par for the course, there were problems
with Sariandi's find. While initial analysis at Moscow
University apparently confirmed the archaeologist's
claims, on two other occasions, samples of the sediments
sent to labs in the late 1990s and early 2000s failed to
detect poppy, ephedra or cannabis. The supposed cannabis
was instead thought to be millet. It was also suggested
that if poppy seeds were present, they could have come
from field weeds or were being used in food rather than
as an opiate.[58] There are also many issues with Soma as
cannabis, including the fact that it grows everywhere in
India, its stalks are woody and not the psychoactive part
of the plant,[59] and in the time of the Rig Veda, people
in India only used hemp for ropes.[60] Sariandi responded
by saying the latter samples he sent had been exposed to
the elements for five years and therefore had lost their

integrity. All of these doubts clouded Sariandi's claim that he had physical evidence of Soma.

F. Max Müller, an Indologist who published an important edition of the Rig Veda, is quoted as saying: 'It is no sign of scientific honesty to attempt to claim for what is in reality a branch of historical research, a character of mathematical certainty . . . it is only the rawest recruit who expects mathematical precision where, from the nature of the case, we must be satisfied with approximate aimings.'[61] Herein lies a fundamental confusion in the arguments to identify Soma. Researchers have tried to apply the scientific rigours of proof to a problem that lacks enough information to settle the debate. Every theory has enough flaws to relegate it to the realm of hypotheses.

The search for the Soma plant has certainly been an interesting exercise in the theory that early religions had entheogenic roots, and it has spurred a greater understanding of the psychoactive and therapeutic properties of South Asian plants. Such explorations for and speculation about crypto-plants are not new and account for a subgenre of ethnobotany, with researchers dissecting and publicly debating the identities of inebriating plants used in religious or literary texts.[62] Academics have attempted to name the plants used for *nepenthe*, the 'drug of forgetfulness' in the Odyssey, and *kykeon*, the drink mentioned in the ancient Greek Eleusinian Mysteries, consumed by members of a Demeter and Persephone cult.

Together, such investigations, including the study of Soma and its effects, serve as a kind of holy grail for understanding the primacy of religion, the meaning of spirituality and attempts to explore the outer edges of human consciousness. In this sense, perhaps the question of what plant produced Soma has led us to larger questions about godliness and the *feeling* of spirit. Why do people seek to transform their consciousness? What was the essence of Soma that its users sought?

IV

In my early twenties, I attended a lecture that my father gave at Carleton College in Northfield, Minnesota. Afterwards, I chatted with one of his colleagues, who told me quite generously that he walked away from every conversation with my father with new ideas, each one large enough to devote many years of study to. AKR recognized the importance of choosing big questions, and Soma is no different. Beneath his Soma poems lies a large body of inquiry. But why such interest in an unanswerable question?

The opening of Doniger's 'Post-Vedic History of the Soma Plant' proposes:

> . . . if one accepts the point of view that the whole of Indian mystical practice from the *Upaniṣads* through the more mechanical methods of yoga is merely an attempt to recapture the vision granted by the Soma plant, then the nature of that vision—and of that plant— underlies the whole of Indian religion, and everything of a mystical nature within that religion is pertinent to the identity of the plant.

As Doniger suggests, this idea stems from the Vedic people migrating from the mountains—where Soma grew—to the plains of the Ganges, after which they no longer had access to it. In order to maintain the ritual, they adopted Soma substitutes, some of which may have approximated the effect while others may not have been entheogenic or even psychoactive at all. But these plants somehow resembled the original Soma, and they could be ceremonially pressed for their sap. Other psychoactive substances could be ruled out: Alcohol was certainly not a substitute, as Soma was drunk the same day it was pressed, so there wasn't time for fermentation; hemp was for rope-making then, not for *bhang*; palm toddy was not pressed; and poppies for opium weren't yet grown in the Indian plains.[63] Around the sixth century BCE, coinciding with these migrations, fasting, yoga, meditation and breathing exercises arose, perhaps as ways to reproduce the mystical experience of Soma through internal, voluntary means because priests could no longer find the sacred plant.[64] According to this theory, having experienced Soma, losing it and seeking replacements may have shaped elements of Hindu culture.

If the adoption of internal practices represents a substitute for the original nectar of the gods, AKR's Soma poems go even further. In the poems, altered consciousness is diffused into life, occurring in fractions. In AKR's interview with Ayyappa Paniker, he talks about 'demythologization' or making an 'entirely mythic character ordinary'. In these poems, Soma is presented as a kind of 'restless' trickster.[65] He is brought to earth; 'once eye / of heaven, now a mushroom at my feet.'[66] AKR writes:

Soma, Soma has no similar,
grows ordinary as mystery,

ancient familiar,
the always here.[67]

In these lines, Soma is one of a kind yet ever-present; ordinary and mysterious; ancient and familiar; intermingling in everyday experience. The poems *are* metaphysical, with heterogeneous ideas yoked together. For Vedic priests, Soma provided a conduit from a mortal, human, earthly realm to an immortal, god-like, expansive spirit world; the Soma poems present a steady drumbeat of a spirit world appearing simultaneously in the mundane.

In 'Wish we could talk about Soma and such', he writes of Soma 'without capitals' and of Vishnu, Siva and Parvati. 'We know them well / we'll know them if we see them anywhere,' the poem reads, familiarizing the deities in pedestrian moments. The poem continues:

We know them from childhood
Wish we could speak of them
Now at fifty,
Without irony, without allegory,
Whenever they occur,
as they do,
in the middle of a thought,
at the corner of 57th Street,[68]
talking about chickens
to a butcher.

AKR removes Soma from ritual and places it within a daily routine. In the Paniker interview, he references his new book of poems, which he says is about 'the presence of whatever one calls "divine" in our ordinary life, that is, the experience that is slightly different from it.'

If one looks at the theorized evolution of the Soma experience, from its original 'drink of the gods' that gifted its consumer with ecstasy, rapture, bliss and immortality to its inspiration for more sedate yet consciousness-altering replacements of yoga and meditation, these poems offer a further dilution. They suggest everyday rifts in baseline reality, the divine that exists in moments, infinitesimal yet new. And doesn't that define poetry itself, using language in new ways to reveal beauty or insight in small moments, creating cracks for us to be 'astonished at ordinary things'?[69]

The secret plant's effects and the elite ritual that only Vedic priests were privy to are democratized in these poems. If the original Soma drink and ceremony were grand departures from ordinary consciousness, these poems seem to say that Soma exists everywhere, at any time, even 'on Friday morning / as the sun splits the thatches / with roof long slits / of skylights'.[70]

Bibliography

Basham, A.L. *The Wonder That Was India.* London: Sidgwick and Jackson, 1954.

Biswas, Jayita, and Rita Singh. 'Ephedra stipitata (Ephedraceae), a new species from Ladakh, India'. *Annales Botanici Fennici* 59, no. 1 (2022): 123–29. https://doi.org/10.5735/085.059.0119.

Clark, Matthew James. *The Tawny One: Soma Haoma and Ayahuasca.* London: Muswell Hill Press, 2017.

Clark, Matthew James. *Botanical Ecstasies: Psychoactive Plant Formulas in India and Beyond.* London: Psychedelic Press, 2021.

Doniger, Wendy. *The Rig Veda: An Anthology of One Hundred and Eight Hymns.* London: Penguin Books, 1981.

Doniger, Wendy. *The Hindus: An Alternative History.* New York: Penguin Press, 2009.

Falk, Harry. 'Soma I and II'. *Bulletin of the School of Oriental and African Studies* 52, no. 1 (1989): 77–90.

Flattery, David Strophlet, and Martin Schwarz. *Haoma and Harmaline. The Botanical Identity of the Indo–Iranian Hallucinogen 'Soma' and its Legacy in Religion, Language and Middle Eastern Folklore.* Near Eastern Studies, vol. 21. Berkeley/Los Angeles/London: University of California Press, 1989.

Houben, Jan E.M. 'The Soma–Haoma problem: Introductory overview and observations on the discussion'. *Electronic Journal of Vedic Studies*, vol. 9, no. 1 (2003): 1-35.

Hummel, Karl. 'Review of Wasson 1969'. *Studien zur Indologie und Iranistik*, vol. 20 (1997): 79–90.

Macdonell, Arthur Anthony. *Hymns from the Rigveda.* Calcutta: Association Press, 1922. http://www.archive.org/details/cu31924023014750.

McDonald, Andrew. 'A Botanical Perspective on the Identity of Soma (Nelumbo Nucifera Gaertn.) Based on Scriptural and Iconographic Records'. *Economic Botany* 58, December (2004): 147–73.

McKenna, Terence K. *Food of the Gods: The Search for the Original Tree of Knowledge: A Radical History of Plants, Drugs, and Human Evolution.* New York, NY: Bantam Books, 1992.

Miller, Richard J. 'Religion as a Product of Psychotropic Drug Use'. *The Atlantic.* Dec. 27 (2013).

Miller, Richard J. *Drugged: The Science and Culture behind Psychotropic Drugs.* New York, NY: Oxford University Press, 2014.

Merlin, M.D. 'Archaeological Evidence for the Tradition of Psychoactive Plant Use in the Old World'. *Economic Botany* 57, no. 3 (2003): 295–323. http://www.jstor.org/stable/4256701.

O'Flaherty, Wendy Doniger. 'The Post-Vedic History of the Soma Plant'. In R. Gordon Wasson, *Soma: Divine Mushroom of Immortality*. New York: Harcourt Brace Jovanovich, 1971.

Pollan, Michael. *How to Change Your Mind*. New York: Penguin, 2018.

Paudel, Keshav Raj, and Nisha Panth. 'Phytochemical Profile and Biological Activity of Nelumbo nucifera'. *Evidence-Based Complementary and Alternative Medicine*, vol. 2015, Article ID 789124, 16 pages, 2015. https://doi.org/10.1155/2015/789124.

Ramanujan, A.K. *Journeys: A Poet's Diary*. Edited by Krishna Ramanujan and Guillermo Rodríguez. Gurgaon: Penguin Random House, 2019.

Ramanujan, A.K. *The Collected Essays of A.K. Ramanujan*. Edited by Vinay Dharwadker. New Delhi: Oxford University Press, 1999.

Riedlinger, Thomas J. 'Wasson's Alternative Candidates for Soma'. *Journal of Psychoactive Drugs* 25, no. 2 (1993): 149–56. doi:10.1080/02791072.1993.10472245.

Rodríguez, Guillermo. *When Mirrors are Windows. A View of A.K. Ramanujan's Poetics*. New Delhi: Oxford University Press, 2016.

Schultes, Richard Evans. 'Hallucinogens of Plant Origin'. *Science* 163, no. 3864 (1969): 245–54. https://doi.org/10.1126/science.163.3864.245.

Sariandi, Victor I. 'Margiana and Soma-Hoama'. *Electronic Journal of Vedic Studies*, Vol. 9, Issue 1c, (2003): pp. 1-20.

Spess, David. *Soma: The Divine Hallucinogen*. Rochester, VT: Park Street Press, 2000.

Staal, Frits. 'How a Psychoactive Substance Becomes a Ritual: The Case of Soma'. *Social Research* 68 (3), (2001): 745–78.

Wasson, R. Gordon. *Soma: Divine Mushroom of Immortality.* New York: Harcourt Brace Jovanovich, 1968.

The 'Ordinary Mystery' Trip: Soma in A.K. Ramanujan's Poetry

Guillermo Rodríguez

Soma, the juice believed to have been consumed by the Hindu gods and their ancient priests during rituals, was thought to have astonishing properties, as described in one of the Mandalas of the Rig Veda.[1] Taken during ritual sacrifices, it could cure illnesses, bring riches and also inspire artists and poets.

Though there have been many modern theories[2] about which plant Soma may have been derived from, according to Indian mythology, the gods gained their immortality by drinking Soma and it was the favourite beverage of the Vedic god Indra. The Soma drink was personified by the god of the same name; it turned into Soma, the god of sacrifices associated with the moon.

In the historic year of 1968, which is remembered for ushering in more revolutions than the world could digest, and signalled the beginning of a new era in contemporary history, R. Gordon Wasson published a ground-breaking volume: *Soma: Divine Mushroom of Immortality*.[3] This work had an immediate impact on many Indian scholars, writers and poets[4] in America who either read Wasson's book or followed the subsequent debate it stirred. A.K. Ramanujan, who became professor of Dravidian studies and linguistics at the departments of South Asian Languages and Civilizations and Linguistics at the University of Chicago that same year, discovered[5] Soma in a new light thanks to the novel theory propounded by the veteran ethnomycologist and former banker. Ramanujan was thrilled by the modern re-interpretation and contextualization of an old myth, and it spurred his restless poetic imagination to greater depths than he could have then predicted. The glowing image of Soma as a hallucinogenic mushroom remained with AKR throughout the years. In one of his lecture notes on Soma, dated around 1979–80, he writes:

Vedic literature, as Frits Staal[6] pointed out in another context, opposes Agni to Soma, the domestic and the ecstatic, one where Nature is domesticated by Culture through fire (as Levi–Strauss would say). The other where a domestic and social culture is left behind, transcended, by a Plant, a psychedelic mushroom, Soma, [whose] mind-blowing experience itself is later ritualized. As Kafka said in a parable about such structures and anti-structures: Leopards break into the temple and drink of the holy water; if it happens often enough, leopards become part of the ceremony. This Agni/Soma contrast is seen in mythology as Visnu and Siva, in the texts in the transition from the Vedas to the Upanishads and Aranyakas.[7]

Soma is cited in the Vedas as a plant, a drug and a god, the 'lord of speech, leader of poets, and seer among priests'.[8] The notion of an external force or elixir 'inspiring' or 'possessing' poets, both a drug and a god—*Soma*, as the ancient Hindus called it—captivated AKR's creativity for at least over a decade. From around 1971 to 1982, he was deeply involved, artistically and intellectually, with developing his personal idea of Soma: not just as a metaphor for the ecstatic or for a special state of being, but as an exploration of what any perceptive mind (and poet in the poem) might recognize as commonplace inspiration. This continued attraction included experimentation of various kinds. An experience with the psychedelic mescaline in the summer of 1971, recorded in his notes,[9] produced several pages of prose poetry and erratic verse lines that play with the 'mind-blowing' effects of the drug on his sense impressions. What began as a personal and artistic experiment, also with poetic forms, slowly turned into a body of poems. By 1980–82, several manuscripts titled 'Soma' as well as other scattered 'Soma Poems' were being stored in his files. He even announced in those years, in several interviews,[10] that he intended to bring out a new poetry collection under that title. But the 'Soma' collection was never published.

The period from the early 1970s to the early 1980s also coincides with an important chapter in Indian literary history. Indian poetry in English was gaining general acceptance and publications were flourishing in India[11] but this new wave of interest in Indian poets did not coincide with a new volume of poetry in English by AKR. There is a long gap between the publication of *Relations* (1971), his second book of poems after *The Striders*

(1966), and the third collection, *Second Sight* (1986). Or so it seems, since AKR's unrelenting creativity was steered towards his translational work in those years, with several pioneering works being published that became undisputable classics: *Speaking of Siva*, a collection of medieval Kannada bhakti poems from the Vīrasaiva tradition, published in 1973; his translation of the highly influential and ground-breaking novel *Samskara* by U.R. Anantamurthy in 1976, and his passionate translations of the Tamil Āḻvār poetry, *Hymns for the Drowning: Poems for Visnu by Nammāḻvār* published in 1981.[12]

So what does the 'Soma period' signify in AKR's career as a poet writing in English? As a poetry project, 'Soma' was for this south Indian professor living in the crisis-ridden America of the 1970s above all an attempt at 'demythologization' that carried with it a fatality and a healthy dose of irony. It was meant as a personal coming-to-terms with poetry as religion, which is a profound universal theme. The play with religious and mythological connotations helped him take an ironic distance from the ancient classical sources as well as from a new breed of mystics and gurus.[13] AKR adopted a pseudo-religious personal voice that was modern and secular. He was responding creatively, in his own terms, with what we may define (in his own critical parlance) as a 'counter-text' to the Sanskrit tradition. Just as, a few years earlier, his well-known ironic poem 'Prayer to Lord Murugan'[14] stood as a poetic counter-text to the classical Tamil tradition.[15]

Thus, the concept of Soma has profound implications for AKR's aesthetics and poetics[16] and is rooted in his intellectual history and personal use of Sanskrit myths and motifs. We find in his writings on Soma (prose as well as poetry) as much a de-mythologization as a deconstruction of the concept—an inquiry from the point of view of the multiple traditions—pan-Indian (Sanskritic), regional (bhakti and oral), and Western—that fed into his system of thought and expression.

Soma is often referred to as the source of creative imagination, and in AKR's associations, it covers a wide semantic territory: physical, metaphysical, psychedelic, mythological, religious, literary and autobiographical. As a personal metaphor, it has multiple overlapping connotations: the mind, the soul (versus the body), the self or *jivatman*, inspiration or inspired consciousness, a mythological god-figure or substance, a symbolic motif of the moon, or an elixir, 'food of the god', a mushroom, a drug and anti-structure. These are the interrelated layers of meaning that reverberate in the background of AKR's 'Soma poems'. For the sake of providing an overview, these multiple threads can be placed under four main categories:

i   Autobiographical circumstances
ii Modern cultural and literary contexts (western and Indian postcolonial)
iii Classical Indian Sanskrit traditions: Vedas, Brahmanas, Upanishads, etc.
iv Vīrasaiva and Ālvār medieval bhakti traditions related to the notions of rebirth, inspiration, possession, etc.

In this essay, I shall briefly touch on these interrelated components that converge in the Soma poems.

The early 1970s were filled with episodes of personal turmoil for AKR. In 1971, he divorced his spouse, Molly, who moved to Delhi with their two children. Depressed, he resorted to marijuana at times and tried mescaline in Madison in August, alone in a friend's apartment. During the experience with the drug, he scribbled notes and verse lines that he later marked as 'Mescalin Notes' (28–29 August 1971) in his files.[17] In these notes, AKR refers to Huxley as well as to Samkhya philosophy, the Hindu concepts of rebirth and continuity through change, etc., and cites, for instance, the medieval Vīrasaiva woman saint Akkamahadevi and her vacanas on endless rebirth. The mescaline trip is described as an experiential tour de force, as he relates to the outer world and its external stimuli both as a heightened aesthetic awareness and as an existential search for an 'inner truth', which springs from this contrasting experience of the physical—the body—versus an 'out of body' consciousness. It is quite astounding how, even at the height of the drug's effects, AKR is able to jot down his sense impressions and visions as he keeps up the pace of writing in this mad, flowing free-association, in an unstoppable stream of (dream-) consciousness. A good deal of his prose and poetry from the 1970s embodies these visions and represents the fluctuation between wakefulness and the dream world (or māyā), that is, the dualities of structure and variation (in linguistics), solidity and fluidity, fixity and dissolution, which are equally present in the poetry of the Āḻvārs.

In the 1970s, AKR often searched for answers and inspiration in the south Indian mystics and he worked intensely on poetry translations from medieval Kannada and Tamil. In *Speaking of Siva* (1973), he breathes new life into the revolutionary Kannada Vīrasaiva poets he had 'discovered' as a student in his native Mysore in the mid-1940s. And from 1976 onwards, he immersed himself in the Vaishnavite Āḻvār poetry while he was translating the *Tiruvāymoḻi* by Nammāḻvār[18] at Carlton College, Northfield, Minnesota, where he had moved in 1975 after reuniting with his family. The Āḻvār poets, as we can see in several examples, made him yearn for a poetry of 'possession' and 'connections' to the extent that he was tempted to merge his verse with the mystical south Indian bards.

Thus, AKR 'contextualized' his interest in hallucinogenic experiments and translated their psychological–philosophical imports into his own multicultural condition: as a Hindu (Brahmin) exploring the Vedic root of 'Soma', as a Kannadiga steeped in the oral vacana tradition and as a Vaishnavite of Tamil origin. Just as peyote is and was used by the Mexican native priests (shamans) to 'talk to God', he knew since childhood that the Brahmins used Soma as their divine drink. But Soma as 'Lord of Speech' reminded him much later of the medieval mystical poetries, in particular the Āḻvār poems he studied closely, in which it is the god Vishnu that 'possesses' the poet. And this suddenly became, for a mature man already in his forties, a (revolutionary) model to embrace and adapt to his own needs, and also to translate; just like the more radical Siva-worshipping Lingayat poets in Kannada had been in his teenage years, a paradigm of anti-structure that broke social and artistic conventions. In his lecture 'Men, Women, Saints' delivered in 1976 at Harvard University,[19] the year he was working on some of the early Soma drafts as well as on the Āḻvār translations, AKR describes the Soma concept in the context of the Vedas as a 'psychedelic juice': 'Soma . . . is

psychedelic, mind-blowing, not exactly social—probably
a sacred mushroom, a juice for which maybe the body
itself is the ultimate filter. It is part of the ecstatic religion
of the time, not easily contained by social arrangements.'

An interest in mescaline, peyote (a cactus), mushrooms,
LSD and other hallucinogenic substances was common
in the liberated social milieu of American artists and
writers,[20] as the hippie culture of the 1960s followed the
excesses of the pioneering Beat poets. The word 'soma'
had gained notoriety in the West after the publication of
Aldous Huxley's *Brave New World* in 1932. In this famous
book, 'Soma' is used in a pejorative sense to denote the
drug that keeps the populace of the 'new world' under
control. As a confluence of life, science, art, poetry and
philosophy, Huxley's psychedelic experiments described
in *The Doors of Perception* (1954) partly inspired Allen
Ginsberg[21] and the poets of the Beat Generation to try out
hallucinogenic mushrooms, LSD and other substances.

Nonetheless, in his Soma Poems, AKR wanted to
show how poetry is different both from divine inspiration
and from the psychedelic drug-induced experience in
that it 'works' exactly like ordinary life. So, rather than
considering himself a 'mystical opportunist'[22] like the
Vīrasaiva saints or having to resort to intoxicating drugs,
AKR developed a pragmatic attitude to art and life
through the habit of saying 'no to nothing', be it food,
women, or poems.[23] His concept of inspiration, or 'grace',
as he preferred to call it, does not recognize a superior
force but rather sees art as an interruption of routine life.
In an interview conducted in 1980, he explains poetic
inspiration, therefore, in paradoxical terms as an ordinary
mystery:

> Poetry happens unbidden and has to protect itself. The psychedelic experience taps precisely such experiences. But the junkies seek it as a separate state and not as an interruption of the ordinary . . . Perhaps that is what grace is all about. And this is where the ironic distance comes in. My point is, you can't seek such a state, can't organize it or take a pill for it. In my 'Soma Poems', for instance, the extraordinary occurs in a most ordinary fashion, something like the way a poem happens. It's a mystery, but mystery itself is ordinary. Only we make of it something miraculous.[24]

AKR further discussed his Soma poems in two other interviews published between 1981–82. Literary critic Chirantan Kulshrestha comments in the introduction to his edited conversation with AKR: 'The drafts are very unlike the poems Ramanujan has published earlier; still, they bear, in a turn of phrase or in the particulars of an image, his unmistakable signature. There is a marvelous sequence of "soma" poems which adopt non-realistic means to cope with stubborn realities . . .'[25] And a year later, in the interview with Ayyappa Paniker, AKR repeats his mantra of the quotidian opportunist in poetic 'grace', a paradoxical condition that was critical to his life and poetry: '. . . the presence of whatever one calls "divine" in our ordinary life, that is, the experience that is slightly different from it. My new book of poems in English is also about that paradox. I am going to call it Soma.'[26]

In AKR's Soma poems, the multiple connotations of Soma (as the intoxicating substance from the Vedas, as food, moon, mythological god(s) that inspire poets, as well as personal metaphor for the inspired poet) appear in a metonymical relation. The drug-elixir 'given' by the god, that is, poetry, is the means to invoke 'the seer and leader of poets', and thus the poet's creativity is an extension of his grace. The poet sees through 'Soma' and takes on different identities. The drug and god are both the sources of inspiration and the explanation for it. Depending on the attitude (aesthetic or philosophical) and personal belief (secular or religious), it may have diverse interpretations, from the physical and metaphysical to the psychedelic and religious. The poet, the muse and the 'divine' experience in ordinary life, as well as the poem, are part of the same circle of poetic creation and (self-)reflection. And this is precisely the elusive centre piece in the puzzle of AKR's fluid poetics. His aesthetic belief[27] is, in practice, also continuity through transformation: there is no fixed centre, no secure self, no single-faced portrait, as it always changes; it is a composite form, as in a mirror game of reflections and illusions. Thus, AKR often highlights the arbitrariness of 'Soma', which can be poetry, the poet, the persona, or the person in search of poems.

Let us now have a closer look at a few of the poems in the enigmatic 'Soma' series, a group of poems that reflect on the creative self and 'talk' to each other, to earlier drafts, and to the poet's translations of ancient mystics. In AKR's oeuvre, sometimes similar poems coexist as variations or keep changing titles with new adjustments. As he concedes in the Paniker interview, different versions 'can survive', as he thought of them as 'related poems, poems of the same family'. The first poem in the present volume has been placed ad hoc as a curtain-raiser and invocation:

Soma is restless.
Grab him, he breaks away.
When he moves through the world,
as a hand through the cloud,
the blind man sees, the lame step forth.
You rush at evil,
enemy of enemies;
help us seek and help us find
what we seek,
and find and see
half what we lost before.

Be kind, Soma.
Do not confuse our little flowers with your
whirl of skills.
Do not spear our cells with light.
Do not put us in a rage, nor in a terror.
Help us see as you see,
the evil of the gods in the house.

The original manuscript of this poem was handwritten and carried the puzzling title 'Soma (121)'. When reading this draft after the other Soma poems, I found it strikingly different. The poem introduces us to Soma's magical (but personified) qualities and we learn about his astounding powers. We hear the poet first addressing, then pleading with, the god. The verses bear a ritualistic aura and lack the ironic stance and modern flavour that came with the other Soma poems. Though it was clearly a first draft, with several edits and deletions, it had a structural unity and conscious rhythmic pattern, very much like the style of the Soma Hymns in the *Rig Veda*. After some speculation,

I identified it as AKR's own free adaptation (a second, modernized echo) of Wendy Doniger's translation of Rig Veda 8.79 published in 1981.[28] What gave its source away was the number in brackets after the title 'Soma': it referred to the page number in Doniger's book (121).

A handful of lines in the Soma poems can be traced directly to the rough drafts in the 'Mescalin Notes'. Whatever the direct and indirect connections of the mescaline episode to particular poems may be, the traces of hallucinogenic experiences are unmistakably present in several other published poems by AKR and in his prose. In his Kannada novella *Mathobbana Atmacharitre* (Someone Else's Autobiography) for instance, the narrator describes the aftershocks of 'someone else's' LSD trip:

Dormant feelings of this kind might suddenly burst forth years later, when least expected: perhaps, while taking a piss off a road in Germany or Mysore, or while looking at the iridescence of piss, or while noticing the gleam in the eyes reflected in a bathroom mirror. To the dismay of one's wife and children, such unsettling confusions are likely to linger for hours and days.[29]

In the last pages of the 'Mescalin Notes', AKR scribbled dozens of tentative 'poems' and observations, for he felt it was 'somehow important to register, record everything still' as the images continued to rush to his mind on Sunday morning:

Like my son I held my
peepee and played garden hose in the bathtub
and like my grandson

I was unborn.

....

Aug 29
10:40 A bath
Mind still popping with 'poems'
Like my grandfather
I bathed before
Like my father
I slapped soap
on my back
Like me
I rubbed myself
with a Sears turkey—
towel[30]

One of the clearest pieces of evidence of how the mescaline experience got transformed into a published poem is 'Extended Family', which made it to *Second Sight*. The 'I' in this composition muses poignantly (during a 'bath') over the Hindu concept of family and the chain of rebirths:

Extended Family

Yet like grandfather
I bathe before the village crow
the dry chlorine water
my only Ganges
the naked Chicago bulb
a cousin of the Vedic sun
slap soap on my back
like father

and think
in proverbs
like me
I wipe myself dry
when mirrors are windows
with an unwashed
Sears turkish towel

....

I hold my peepee
like my little son
play garden hose
in and out
the bathtub
like my grandson
I look up
unborn
at myself
like my great
great grandson
I am not yet
may never be
my future
dependent
on several
people
yet
to come (1–14, 29–47)[31]

In the mescaline notes, after the playful sequence of
bathing habits replicating through generations of male
family members, there comes the following existential
observation:

> There won't be paper enough—feel like tempting my
>   endurance—and taking
> another dose for this luminous Sun-day and be the
>   sundance kid—praying
> mantis—still on the leaf it's eating, the soul a caterpillar
>   eating leaf after leaf
> and moving to another—[32]

The caterpillar eating on a leaf is a classical Hindu motif for reincarnation from the Upanishads, and a repeated image in AKR's published poetry. It is there, for instance, in the closing lines of the poem 'Elements of Composition', which opens *Second Sight* in 1986. In the Soma collection, it appears in a key passage in another crucial poem: 'On discovering that Soma is a mushroom', which was inspired by Wasson's theory of Soma being the mushroom *Amanita muscaria*:

> Would you believe it?
>
> Soma, once eye of heaven,
> now a mushroom at my feet.
>
> Then I'm a willow tree with fountains
> of falling hair, not this man, whom you and I
> know somewhat, but willow among oaks
>
> in a ring of snow mountains,
> for Soma is a mushroom at my feet.
> Yes, I'm still the same, here and now as always
> married and difficult, a handful

of thumbs with a hammer and nail,
reading a newspaper once a year,
living at two
addresses, office and home,
you or he or even I can write to,

though Soma is a mushroom growing at my feet.
Wedded to doubt and married to a woman,
now man now willow with falling hair
and two addresses, two children,
six and eight, girl and boy, in a ring
of mountains, reading a newspaper

on a staircase spiral as if in Istanbul
in Mustafa's place, for Soma's me,
mushroom, ancient of altitudes,
growing at my feet.   Soma of seven minds,
single phallic eye, glow of red, tremor of drum,
behind eye and ear, growing on the line
between left and right,

bud of the thousand petal lotus in the brain.
Soma, I sit on Soma, caterpillar
on toadstool in the looking-glass world,
eating what I sit on and waiting to be butterfly;
stand in Soma, warm perishing body
in a cold silver river, the water
is a lover's hand,
in, on, below, between,

and Soma growing at my feet.
It's Soma who reads the timeless almanacs

in *The Sun Times* once a year,
photographs the rainbows and auras
all around the black cat and him and you,
sees distant famine in a present meal,
is astonished at ordinary things,

his own breath in winter or the incalculable weight
of a pebble; looks at pecking chicken
and sees only bone-cage
and butcher.   For Soma, October rain
in his floppy shoe
is Indra, gambler god of rain,

the hail a throw of angry dice
at peasants.   Only Soma can talk
of Soma without irony or melodrama,
come, go, and come again,
while you and I go on for some years,

here and now as always
till there's no more now,
wedded to doubt and married to a woman,
wincing at Soma,

embarrassed at Indra
sprouting like this
on my ordinary

English page,
like Soma,

this mushroom at my feet.

In an earlier version (titled simply 'Soma')[33] of this
autobiographical poem drafted in 1979, 'this man'
appears less concealed as 'R.' and the ages of the 'girl
and boy' match those of his actual children then (16 and
14). 'On discovering that Soma is a mushroom' also tells
its 'story' through its form, that is, its verse structure. A
common device in many of AKR's poems, particularly in
his first two collections in English[34] that were influenced
by the imagists, was to play with the shape of a poem and
its verse lines.[35] AKR was also fond of proverbs, riddles
and traditional games. In this poem, lines and numbers
matter very much indeed. The intentionally odd structural
pattern of this composition is evident in the atypical (for
AKR) syntactical breaks and blank spaces within several
of the lines highlighting the word 'Soma':

> growing at my feet.   Soma of seven (14)
>
> --
>
> and butcher.   For Soma, October rain (36)
>
> --
>
> at peasants.   Only Soma can talk (40)
>
> --

There are also unusual short lines, such as 'living at two'
(13). All of this is part of a design. AKR shaped this poem
to convey an image and an idea, subtly hidden, embedded
in the poem. He chose for it a convex stanzaic pattern:
the length of stanzas increases from one line to couplet
to tercet and so on up to an octave and then decreases in
an equal manner back to one line. So the poem, like the
mushroom, 'grows' at his feet as the number of verse lines
in a stanza rises ('growing on the line/between left and

right') and then diminishes in an inverse pattern. Without resorting to a visual shape (varying line lengths around a central axis, as in the tree poem 'A Poem on Particulars'), it has a convex shape, bulging symmetrically, like a mushroom, a tree, a mountain or 'phallic eye'. The poem also conveys the notion of physical contraries: 'heaven', 'altitude', 'mountains', 'staircase spiral', versus 'feet' and 'falling'. Notice the repetition of growing 'at my feet' (reiterated throughout like a mantra), as Soma, once a powerful 'eye of heaven' (the moon) and Vedic plant from the Himalayan mountains, has now been downgraded to a vegetable on the ground at his feet. And it reflects on what is flowing between, as well as above and below: the longest stanza (an octave) ends with the dream-like image of the speaker merging with Soma (the moon-reflection), standing 'in a cold silver river, / the water / is a lover's hand / in, on, below, between'.[36] At the 'subconscious' conceptual level, the poem reminds us of the effect that hallucinogenic mushrooms produce: you get 'high', but the elevating effect doesn't last long, as you 'fall' back on your feet. This is another typical AKR theme and technique used in poems such as 'Highway Stripper' or the earlier iconic poem 'Poem on Particulars' on an orange tree, but it is also concealed in 'Snakes' which plays on the idea of maya or illusion. AKR's poetry—and life—abounds with such highs and lows, ladders and falls.[37] And so, in this 'ordinary' fashion, we experience Soma/inspiration 'come, go, and come again', like a wave, as we see a poem 'sprouting like this / on my ordinary English page, / like Soma, / a mushroom at my feet'.

But let's not forget we have the caterpillar sitting on the Soma-toadstool, getting 'high' on the octave stanza, 'growing on the line', yearning to be a butterfly, eating what it sits on. It is no hookah-smoking caterpillar in Wonderland, yet it is also seeking transmigration in the 'looking-glass world'. Like Alice[38] climbing through the mirror to find everything in reverse, the 'I' in this mirror poem is about to start its trip, descending from convex octave lines into his own 'mind-blowing' dream waters:

> bud of the thousand petal lotus in the brain.
> Soma, I sit on Soma, caterpillar
> on toadstool in the looking-glass world,
> eating what I sit on and waiting to be butterfly;
> stand in Soma, warm perishing body
> in a cold silver river, the water
> ....

In several other Soma poems drafted years after the mescaline experiment, there is a strong underlying sense that particular mental states are bestowed and derive from an outer source. Such poems play with the relation between 'ordinary' inspiration and a superior power and acknowledge different kinds of 'grace', contrasting the old models of spiritual 'takeovers' with the modern, pragmatic view of life from an ironic perspective. I shall give a few examples of this play, which also involves a creative, open dialogue between AKR the poet and AKR the translator and, at times, a merging of the two. An older version of the poem 'Soma' (the second poem in this volume) ends with an inserted line from a poem by the ninth-century poet–saint Nammālvār:

Jazz Poem for Soma

Soma? Why talk of Soma?
Soma's no Vishnu, no Shiva.

More like you, or even me,
no lotus no water can wet,

no third eye, no Lakshmi: for all his fame,
he can churn no sea, turn no mountain, burn

no forest; only lurk in, work on,
lies, eyes, ears, fears, and the rest

of your twenty-four senses.

Then every pore, hair, cell, and muscle,
a body of pleasure with a vein

of pain, a sac of smells
skunk, civet cat, grandma's armpit,

woods that burn and bloom, and other such
bearers of myrrh and frankincense.

Then jails have icicle rows, crystal carrots
slum forsythias have April tongues.

The great ladder now has rungs,
and my world, my mongoloid baby,

has wedding rings on all her ten fingers
and on her thirteen perfect toes.

Soma, Soma has no mimic similar,
no similitude, grows ordinary

as mystery, ancient familiar,
the always here.   Soma's the same

as you, and you, and you, when you make
the right mistake, fall to the ground,

and find your altitude.

So,
poets beware.[39]

This early version of the 'Soma' poem ends with a caveat to readers, i.e., 'poets', to 'beware'. AKR is quoting here the first words from his translation of the famous Nammāḻvār poem on a devotee's 'possession'. But the voice of the improvised 'jazz poem' is wary of delivering the saintly verses beyond the first line. It is only a warning to others and to every prospective reader (and potential 'poet') to be alert to 'the always here', that 'grows ordinary as mystery'. And it is a word of caution to himself, lest he *become* a 'thief / a cheat' by appropriating the poem he translated and, in turn, get 'possessed' by invoking the poet–saint. He heeds the warning—'poets beware' and does not (yet) allow the ancient bard to arrive on the scene and speak through his 'own' poem.

But in a later version, he lets the genie out of the lamp, and the result is a metapoetic 'mutual cannibalism'.[40] In this metonymical relation, it is hard to tell the translator poet from the devotee, as they seem to be 'devoured' by the

god in a process of self-realization. The translated poem
enters the 'flesh' of the composition, and takes over after
the opening lines; the two voices 'sing' now in one voice,
as if proclaiming: 'I' am Soma, now Visnu, the master
of illusions, now *translating* 'my [his] breath, / . . . into
him [my] self'.

> Soma, I said, is no Visnu
> But Visnu can play Soma,
> enter the nests of flesh
> to make them sing:
>
> *Poets,*
> *   beware, your life is in danger:*
>
> *the lord of gardens is a thief,*
> *a cheat,*
> *   master of illusions;*
>
> *he came to me,*
> *   a wizard with words,*
> *   sneaked into my body,*
> *my breath,*
>
> *with bystanders looking on*
> *   but seeing nothing,*
> *he consumed me*
> *   life and limb,*
>
> *and filled me,*
> *   made me over*
> *   into himself*

AKR had translated this Āḻvār poem[41] in the late 1970s. In a note next to this composite poem–translation, Ramanujan defines 'Soma' as the 'moments of insight, joy, sorrow, when we are besides ourselves'.[42] He wanted to use the traditional patterns of devotional poetry to write an extended metapoetic work, a statement on his self-reflecting 'moments' of anxiety, frustration and inspiration as a 'devotee' of poetry.

Such a possession ritual is in line with the Vedic tradition of visionary poets and their use of Soma as the 'lord of speech'. In the poetry of possession, the poem, poet and object of devotion become interchangeable elements and play out a container–contained relationship: the poem is contained by the poet–speaker, who is taken over by the divine genius to consummate the poem, that is, the possession. God, the world, and the devotee stand in a metonymical relationship that is typically expressed on the physical plane of partaking. In this process of 'mutual cannibalism', as AKR described it, god can be both the eater and eaten many times over. In the Soma collection, there are in fact two poems that formally 'embody' the poetry of possession and grace, referring to Soma in a mythological sense and incorporating AKR's own translations. One is the poem by the Vaishnavite Nammāḻvār; in the other instance, 'Yet Siva is sometimes Soma', the poet borrows verses from Māṇikkavācakar, a ninth-century Shaivite, who does not make him 'sing', but 'cry aloud' in 'ecstasy'.[43]

Ever since his encounter with Vīrasaiva bhakti poetry in Mysore in his rebellious youth, AKR was obsessed with the notion of grace and its relation to poetic inspiration. Nammāḻvār's poetry taught him to see that the answer lies 'in the very nature' of human existence, and of poetry, for that matter. The extraordinary moment of grace that all devotees as well as poets patiently crave for and secretly work for requires an occasion that sometimes comes as an 'accident'. For Nammālvār (and AKR identifies here with the Tamil saint), the main obstacle to receiving the grace of 'sharing' with god and of writing good poetry is self-consciousness: 'When Nammālvār speaks of the Lord there is no self-consciousness because the Lord was no stranger to him. The poet should not be self-conscious about using myths or legends or whatever. If he is, he is something less than a poet.'[44] It is precisely this self-consciousness that may have condemned some of AKR's abandoned Soma poems. In his diaries, he occasionally expressed his lack of confidence and inspiration during the years of his Soma experiments. Most of the drafts from this sequence remained unpublished as creative dialogues with the mystics he translated. In the 1982 interview with Paniker, AKR confessed the reasoning behind the title he chose for the book of Nammālvār translations:

Because the word 'al' in 'ālvār' means 'to drown', as well as 'to sink', as well as 'to immerse'. So it's not his body that drowns, though I make a distinction between being immersed and being drowned. And also there is the notion that the immersed ones are talking to the ones who are drowning. They know how to manage it in some way, they have to survive, they have to become alive through the immersion, whereas the rest of us simply drown. That's why I call it *Hymns for the Drowning*.

. . . [O]ne also surrendering to the element, in a way, and not fighting it and so on is also part of it. The poems are full of these situations. There is also one particular poem where the Āḻvār is literally drowning and the Lord comes and saves him. So there are different possibilities for that. People might think that I have stretched the word a bit, but I think it's a nice title. So, it's not the Āḻvārs who are drowning, though there is a poem about the Āḻvār drowning, but I think it's also the reader. Because they talk a great deal about that, about saving the reader.

In the Soma poems, AKR talks half-heartedly about saving himself and finding a 'solution' (often in his distinctive self-mocking style) for his anxieties, preoccupations and poetry writing, but the poems are also about sharing insights, dreams, secrets, riddles and 'happenings' with the reader, whom he regards as his equal. Another intriguing, cryptic composition titled 'When Soma is abroad' is an ironic prayer for his fellow Indian poets writing in English:

When Soma is abroad
dialect and jargon glow.
Mother-tongues wear classics on their sleeves,
father tongues loosen,
schoolbook rules run into love and war,
metres breathe, a mountain breeze
or lion cubs
around a majestic father-theme.

Soma, blow again on the coals of Ezekiel's lips,

make chariots of war pirouette among arrows,
bring medicine men in Delhi offices the red robes of
    shamans,
dawn again on the stones of Jejuri
and circle the squares of Konarak.

The meta-poem on Indian poets and the act of poetry writing is about being 'abroad', understood literally and metaphorically. About living and/or writing in a 'foreign' language and transacting between languages, cultures, territories or countries. Just as AKR worked at the University of Chicago on his 'mother tongues' (Kannada and Tamil) through his father tongue (English),[45] and translated classical Tamil poems of 'love' and 'war',[46] in the second stanza the poetic voice refers in a riddle-like mode to some of India's contemporary poets who wrote in English. He frequently discussed poetry writing and translation with Nissim Ezekiel, P. Lal, Gieve Patel, Arun Kolatkar, Shiv K. Kumar, R. Parthasarathy and others. AKR, who had been in the U.S. since he was a young Fulbright scholar in 1959 (aged thirty), felt that being abroad, taking a distance, helped him (and others) get a new perspective on their mother-tongue traditions (regional languages) as opposed to the father-tongue traditions (English, Sanskrit). And he believed that the act of translating from and writing in the mother-tongue traditions would inspire Indian poets writing in English, help them expand their horizons and enrich their use of language(s). By translating and writing creatively in other languages, poets would contribute to their literary traditions and regional cultures while renewing their own art. Of course, a lot of this 'credo' AKR had imbibed much earlier from T.S. Eliot's writings, and as a professor of English in India, but he had begun practising it in earnest when, as a professor of Dravidian Studies at the University of Chicago, he 'discovered' the literary treasures of his own classical Tamil heritage. He translated out of 'envy',[47] and dreamt about summoning, in modern-day Chicago, Madras, Bombay or Kolkata the fraternity of Sangam poets. And so, in his numerous letters to fellow Indian (mostly multilingual) poets writing in English, he encourages them to translate the Indian classics as well as oral traditions, organize translation workshops and write and publish in their regional languages.

At some point in 1982, AKR started to transform the Soma project and dropped it as it was, unsure of its poetic import as a whole and, to some extent, anxious about the prospect of readers and critics associating his new work with his own life in America or mistaking its multi-layered theme—Soma—with Aldous Huxley's use of the term. He decided to tone down the autobiographical components of the Soma poems, changed some of the titles, transformed a number of poems, and abandoned other drafts altogether. However, there may not have been a single reason for him to discard the Soma sequence as a collection to be published under that title. He also started to have doubts about his Soma poems after re-reading his older 1960s poems. Once more, he wanted to experiment and explore new layers of material and forms by attempting old writing 'exercises' before going ahead with a new poetry publication. On 6 May 1982, he writes: 'Was also surprised by how well-crafted my earlier pieces sounded. Few of my new pieces seem as strong. Maybe I should wait and write some more, before I publish this volume

I'm planning. It's ten years since I've published a book of English poems. Must try some of my own exercises.'[48] Whatever his motives behind this change, from 1982 onwards, AKR started concentrating on a new project he called 'Composition', which explored the multiple meanings of this expression. It integrated many of his earlier concerns with the body and the senses, Whitman's and Hindu philosophical ideas, rebirth, the Upanishads, Buddhism, psychoanalysis and free association, and was, again, distinctly metapoetic. It was also influenced by classical Tamil poetic techniques. He had just concluded his translations for *Hymns for the Drowning* published in 1981, and immediately resumed his translation work of classical Tamil poetry, which resulted in *Poems of Love and War* (1985).

And so the Soma poems mark a transitional phase between AKR's earlier poetry of the 1950s and 1960s, which was highly imagistic, and his later mature poetry of the 1980s, which was more metaphysical, abstract and metapoetic. His imagistic period was influenced by New Criticism (and its stress on craft and form and modernist irony) and by the conversational style of the medieval Kannada vacana poets. The later AKR was shaped not only by the Āḻvār poets but increasingly by the Upanishads. His poetic vision expanded from the body–Soma personal relation to the larger Body–Universe consciousness. The 'Elements of Composition' became a reflection of (and on) 'creation', i.e., life and poetry. The Upanishadic caterpillar motif, food-cycle poems, Whitman's notion of the poetic 'I' as cosmos, bioenergetics, the natural elements and bodily senses, and an ecological worldview are clearly at the back of the concerns that poured into AKR's new 'Composition'.

We know now that the poet either transformed or discarded many of the Soma drafts, even poems that read as finished pieces. When an artist is at work, one idea turns into another, connecting threads of thought and expressiveness. The new project into which the Soma project incarnated—titled 'Composition', a long piece of many new and some old poems stitched together in couplets imitating the classical Tamil *kural* form—was also not published in that single-form avatar. 'Composition' was later broken up into a series of individual interconnected poems, which became *Second Sight* (1986). Its first poem, 'Elements of Composition' opens with the line: 'Composed as I am, like others.'[49]

Creation is always a process, and for AKR, this artistic flow of ideas and words was primordial. That is, the notion that creation—like water, the source of life—is in, through, with and about movement (for 'the moving ever shall stay').[50] This ancient belief he held on to from his youth matured into an integral part of his poetics and is indeed the central theme of the Soma cycle of poems: poems that inquire, embody and search for a 'source'. Yes, the Soma poems can be taken as epiphanic moments with a mystical, sometimes psychedelic, trance-like quality, but after all, they are 'ordinary', self-effacing 'experiences', experiments captured in words and images, with no larger, 'prophetic' pretensions. As drafts, that is, as earlier 'elements of composition' that were either abandoned, 'preserved', nourished or transformed (digested, as it were), dissolving into a larger pool of images, ideas and forms of expression in *Second Sight*.

Sight and insight, stillness and movement alternate, that is the law of life. At one moment we see 'a thing' through the window; suddenly the light changes; we look into the window–mirror, a 'looking glass', and as we reflect and sink into 'a stream' of thoughts, the 'thing' is no more! Nonetheless, words, poems and stories have their 'particular' truths that weigh in and carry on. In the mirror poem 'The Striders', which opens AKR's very first collection of poems by the same name (published in 1966), an 'ordinary', minuscule, flying water insect[51]—that is, the 'poet' in the poem evoking an image for us readers—perches weightlessly, then 'sits on a landslide of lights' and 'drowns eye-deep[52] into its tiny strip of sky'. Now, does he drown or save the bug (and us)? Let's read it again, without fear:

The Striders

Put away, put away this dream
and search
for certain thin
stemmed, bubble-eyed water bugs.
See them perch
on dry capillary legs
weightless
on the ripple skin
of a stream.

No, not only prophets
walk on water. This bug sits
on a landslide of lights
and drowns eye-
deep
into its tiny strip
of sky.[53]

POEMS

(Selection of drafts from 1972 to 1982)

Soma (121)[1]

(After Rig Veda 8.79)

Soma is restless.
Grab him, he breaks away.
When he moves through the world,
    as a hand through the cloud,
the blind man sees, the lame step forth.
You rush at evil,
enemy of enemies;
help us seek and help us find
what we seek,
and find and see
half what we lost before.

Be kind, Soma.
Do not confuse our little flowers with your
    whirl of skills.
Do not spear our cells with light.
Do not put us in a rage, nor in a terror.
Help us see as you see,
the evil of the gods in the house.

Soma[2]

Soma, Soma is no god.
cannot manage a goddess
has no lotus no water can wet,
no third eye, no Lakshmi,
more like you or even me.

He can churn no sea, burn no forest,
turn no mountain.

All he can do is lurk in,
work on, lies, eyes,
ears, fears, and the rest
of your twenty-four senses.[3]

But when he does, pore and hair invent
a body of pleasure with a vein
of pain, a various sac of smells,
garbage skunk, civet cat, grandma's armpit,
woods that burn and bloom,
and other such bearers

of myrrh and frankincense.

Then jails have icicle rows,
like crystal carrots.
Slum forsythias have April tongues.

The great ladder then has rungs,
and the world, our mongoloid baby,
flashes wedding rings
on all her ten fingers
and happiness
on her thirteen twisted toes.

Soma, Soma has no similar,
grows ordinary as mystery,
ancient familiar,
the always here.

Soma is the same as you
and you, and you,
when you make
the right mistake,
fall to the ground,
and find your altitude.

On discovering that
Soma is a mushroom[4]

Would you believe it?

Soma, once eye of heaven,
now a mushroom at my feet.

Then I'm a willow tree with fountains
of falling hair, not this man, whom you and I
know somewhat, but willow among oaks

in a ring of snow mountains,
for Soma is a mushroom at my feet.
Yes, I'm still the same, here and now as always
married and difficult, a handful

of thumbs with a hammer and nail,
reading a newspaper once a year,
living at two
addresses, office and home,
you or he or even I can write to,

though Soma is a mushroom growing at my feet.
Wedded to doubt and married to a woman,
now man now willow with falling hair
and two addresses, two children,
six and eight, girl and boy, in a ring
of mountains, reading a newspaper

on a staircase spiral as if in Istanbul
in Mustafa's place, for Soma's me,
mushroom, ancient of altitudes,
growing at my feet.   Soma of seven minds,
single phallic eye, glow of red, tremor of drum,
behind eye and ear, growing on the line
between left and right,

bud of the thousand petal lotus in the brain.
Soma, I sit on Soma, caterpillar
on toadstool in the looking-glass world,
eating what I sit on and waiting to be butterfly;
stand in Soma, warm perishing body
in a cold silver river, the water
is a lover's hand,
in, on, below, between,

and Soma growing at my feet.
It's Soma who reads the timeless almanacs
in *The Sun Times*[5] once a year,
photographs the rainbows and auras
all around the black cat and him and you,
sees distant famine in a present meal,
is astonished at ordinary things,

his own breath in winter or the incalculable weight
of a pebble; looks at pecking chicken
and sees only bone-cage
and butcher. For Soma, October rain
in his floppy shoe
is Indra, gambler god of rain,

the hail a throw of angry dice
at peasants.   Only Soma can talk
of Soma without irony or melodrama,
come, go, and come again,
while you and I go on for some years,

here and now as always
till there's no more now,
wedded to doubt and married to a woman,
wincing at Soma,

embarrassed at Indra
sprouting like this
on my ordinary

English page,
like Soma,

this mushroom at my feet.

Yet Siva is sometimes Soma[6]

Soma, I said, is no Siva.
Yet Siva sometimes is Soma,
will grab a man by his smallest hair
and kick him upstairs to heaven
as he did once
the poet whose words were rubies,
making him cry aloud:

> *He grabbed me*
> *lest I go astray*

Wax before an unspent fire,
> *mind melted,*
> *body trembled.*

I bowed, I wept,
> *danced, cried aloud,*
> *I sang, and I praised him.*

Unyielding, as they say,
*   as an elephant's jaw*
*   or a woman's grasp,*
*   was love's unrelenting*
*   seizure.*

Love pierced me
*   like a nail*
*   driven into a green tree.*

Overflowing, I tossed
*   like a sea,*

heart growing tender,
body shivering,

while the world called me Demon!
and laughed at me,
I left shame behind,
took as an ornament
*   the mockery of the local folk.*
Unswerving, I lost my cleverness
in the bewilderment of ecstasy.

Soma, I said, is no Visnu[7]

Soma, I said, is no Visnu
But Visnu can play Soma,
enter the nests of flesh
to make them sing:

Poets,
  beware, your life is in danger:

the lord of gardens is a thief,
        a cheat,
master of illusions;

he came to me,
  a wizard with words,
  sneaked into my body,
        my breath,

with bystanders looking on
    but seeing nothing,
he consumed me

life and limb,

and filled me,
        made me over
    into himself

Wish we could talk about
Soma and such[8]

Wish
we could talk about Soma and such
without embarrassment, without capitals;
about Vishnu,
    fancy lotus in his navel
    and world below world
    in that lotus,
    engrossing you, me,
    and Lakshmi;

about Siva, snakes,
three different eyes,
throat blue-black with the poison of a churning sea,
his Parvati, sons
elephant-face and peacock-man,
and her other self, black, many-limbed as a centipede,
thirsting for demon blood,
queen of poxes, hag of plagues.

We know them well,
we'll know them if we see them anywhere,
in your nightmare,
or in my waking.
We know them from childhood,
wish we could speak of them
now at fifty,
without irony, without allegory,
whenever they occur,
as they do,
in the middle of a thought,
at the corner of 57th Street,
talking about chickens
to a butcher.

Soma: he is converted[9]

With that lash of crimson
I convert and wake open

a naked sanyasi
with a hung-over penis

    young seedless cucumber
    of peace

    chameleon
    who'll change
    no more

    one-eyed god
    who'll incarnate
    no more:

    war widows and barren women
    will worship him
    with holy kitchen ash

A.K. Ramanujan

and red poison oleander

all of it falls off
his celibacy
except a pinch of ash

without a touch
he will fill their wombs
with children who'll have children
fathered by the war dead of all the wars

who return as werewolves
to make hairy babies
for future wars,

on Friday morning
as the sun splits the thatches
with roof-long slits
of skylights.

Soma: he reads a newspaper[10]

Looking for a system,
he finds a wife.
'How anger
breaks down
a man
into children!'

Searching for mankind,
he travels
third class,
a carrier for flu,
bugs and eczema:
lose friends

who fear
all symptoms,
any contact
with any contact
with possible syphilis.

Dreams are full of enemies,
bruises;
his wife scrubs
his chest with rough compassion
and Lysol.

Having no clear conscience
he looks for one
in the morning news.
Bengal finds him guilty
of an early breakfast

of two whole poached eggs.
Attacked and defended
by dying armies,

the wounds find
no blood on him,
only a cupboard
full of unused
band-aids.

O alewives floating
on my poison lake
I wish I could feed myself
to your fellow fish
on my dinnerplate.

Soma: he can neither sit nor go[11]

Cannot stand nor sit
for the returning stillness
of my walking,
the fury of my sitting quiet.

Nor sleep nor wake
from the one-legged sleep
on this frozen Chicago lake
of yachts in full sail,

herons
playing at sages.

Soma: he takes a driving lesson[12]

Wresting with the wrong turn,
I crash into the night
killing with my headlights
a man
                pissing away his one innocence
against a tree

mangling my vision
which will clear only
with another birth,

hounded with whips
through twenty-two,
narrow, medieval

marketplaces
and driving lessons
cycle after cycle

given by that man,
his sap now one
with the blood

of that hackberry tree

Ghost[13]

When I see one,
others see a hundred.
When they see a rush,
a carnival, a million,
why do I see nothing,
or worse, just one:
a singular body, a familiar head?

You'd worry too, wouldn't you, if,
in a whole blasted conference
on Delhi milk and China soybean, in all

that human hair, national
smells and international fragrance,
you saw your previous wife,

intimate enemy,
first love (and hate)
unwilling to be second,

not yet six weeks dead,
but standing tall,
now here now there,
in raw-silk sari, in sandalwood footwear?

Soma: he watches TV[14]

My name's the same
as that one-cheek soldier's
thrower once and survivor now
of mortar bombs, his left
a clean profile,

the right wasted
by photograph shrapnel:
cooked rare
in native sewers,
basted in foreign ovens,

joints eaten by nerve-gas,
bark skin with a blue-
anchor tattoo
will decorate
an Argentine lady's

alligator shoe:
an Irish blast

takes my middle finger
in the bus with others—
it once served well

as a dildo in Munich.
And I duck
at seven-thirty
in Beirut
because my wife is Christian.

But I drink coffee,
eat my runny eggs
and burning toast,
wash my wounds
clean,

wear a nose,
a handful of someone
else's fingers,
put on a body-glove
of decent skin,

my own;
and choose,
as if I could
from my cupboard
of skeletons

and umbrellas,
my one remaining face
for the day's throbbing
strobe lights
and revenue offices.

Soma: Sunstroke[15]

Under meridian heat,
wolf, man and twisted tree
stand on their shadow
and grin like one yellow goat.

Breath for arrow, backbone
for bow, I'm demon
of the dry lung, of dust
on the tongue, bubo
in the groin of the bull.

When the raingod's diamond
axed me at dawn,
glancing off a broken bottle
in the slum window

with half a broken wall,
it unbound the waters

throttled in my year of fever,
released a dynasty

in my throat.

Soma: he is hungry but cannot eat[16]

Hungry,
    he has no appetite
    for eggs,
    seeds, leaves,
    rump-flesh, liver,
    or neck
    of fellow-tree, fellow-fowl
    or fellow-beast.

Thirsty,
    he finds the red
    of the wine slimy
    with the blood of bees,
    the wetness of water
    mossy with the fibre
    of the Canidae worm,
    calves' teeth in the foaming milk
    rattle in his mouth,

and the sugarcane worker's sickle
wheels in the candy,
cuts the palate
slits the tongue.

Soma: he looks into himself[17]

X-rayed by my own
twenty-four senses

a negative skeleton
in a crimson core
a network body
with an orange shadow-tree.

seventy-two pulses
beating in a dinosaur
underbelly

yet a man
looking into the mirror
sees only a man
looking into the mirror

Soma: he looks at autumn leaves[18]

With body after body
sunstruck and moonlit,

amethyst leaves,
half green half yellow,

leaves in the fall
with no fall at all:

the windowpane
has a baby's handprint

from another tenancy,
with rainbow rays

like the necks
of dead pigeons:

the daily body's
diamond bodies

opaque with dazzle:
the leaves are amethyst

with veins of coral

because eyes
are opal:

even I believe

for one whole minute,
in Lakshmi and Vishnu,

the journey
to Ixtlan,[19]

the garden
forever here

though forever lost.

He looks at a broken bottle[20]

Struck on the head
with a diamond axe
glinting from a broken bottle
I lose my head
and come
to my senses.

Shot silk
rustles in my living room,
wild stag in the tall grass,
nostrils choke on burning feather
and the weather turns black
at noon.

I see flies,
phosphorescent flies
in the white eyes
and the red straw hair
of the three children
left behind by a passing famine.

He looks at the Persian rug[21]

A live chicken.
He thinks he can hear it cluck
but it's plucked
when he looks again,

gooseflesh skin
trussed in plastic,
legs up, asshole plugged
with its own neck
and liver,

> like the buffalo
> in the sacrifice,[22]
> a beast clutching
> his broken leg
> between his teeth.

And before he can think
this chicken's a buffalo,
a scapegoat slaughtered

in a village of sins
for the virgin goddess
black hag of plagues.

The frozen chickenstone
shrinks on the block
to an egg
tinier than a robin's,
a frog's,
a mosquito's,
a one-eyed cell
with a wavering wall:
I touch it
and touch only
the grain
of the butcher's woodblock,
zigzag
bloodlines,
knifemarks

of many cleavers,
heartwood
circles
of a square
tree.

When Soma is abroad[23]

When Soma is abroad
dialect and jargon glow.
Mother tongues wear classics on their sleeves,
father tongues loosen,
schoolbook rules run into love and war,
metres breathe, a mountain breeze
or lion cubs
around a majestic father-theme.

Soma, blow again on the coals of Ezekiel's lips,
make chariots of war pirouette among arrows,
bring medicine men in Delhi offices the red robes of
    shamans,
dawn again on the stones of Jejuri
and circle the squares of Konarak.

Extended Family I
(He reads a letter from home)[24]

Blood on the trains
        for a country

barefoot policemen
    shaking their legs
    out of the floating ash
    of uncles and villages
       for a state

fear of elephantiasis
       for a cousin

dysentery
       for a daughter

a wandering dog bite
       for a son

A.K. Ramanujan

a straphanger's severed hand
　　in the lobster oven
　　of a Delhi bus
　　　　for a wife

an art gallery on sale
　　for a house

Extended Family II[25]

Yet like grandfather
I bathe before the village crow

the dry chlorine water
my only Ganges

the naked Chicago bulb
a cousin of the Vedic sun

slap soap on my back
like father

and think
in proverbs

like me
I wipe myself dry

with an unwashed
Sears turkish towel

A.K. Ramanujan

like mother
I hear faint morning song

(though here it sounds
Japanese)

and three clear strings
nextdoor

through kitchen
clatter

like my little daughter
I play shy

hand over crotch
my body not yet full

of thoughts novels
and children

I hold my peepee
like my little son

play garden hose
in and out
the bathtub

like my grandson
I look up

unborn
at myself

like my great
great grandson

I am not yet
may never be

my future
dependent

on several
people

yet
to come

Soma: he thinks of leaving his body (to a hospital)[26]

I know, you told me,
    your nightsoil and all
your city's, goes still
    warm every morning
in a government
    lorry, drippy (you said)
but punctual, by special
    arrangement to the municipal
gardens to make the grass
    grow tall for the cows
in the village, the rhino
    in the zoo: and the oranges
plump and glow, till
    they are a preternatural
orange.

Good animal yet perfect
    citizen, you, you are

biodegradable, you do
    return to nature: you will
your body to the nearest
    hospital, changing death into small
change and spare parts;
    dismantling, not de-
composing like the rest
    of us. Eyes in an eye bank
to blink some day for a stranger's
    brain, wait like mummy wheat
in the singular company
    of single eyes, pickled,
absolute.

Hearts,
            with your kind of temper,
    may even take, make connection
with alien veins, and continue
    your struggle to be naturalized:
beat, and learn to miss a beat
    in a foreign body.
                        But
you know my tribe, incarnate
    unbelievers in bodies,
they'll speak proverbs, contest
    my will, against such degradation.
Hidebound, even worms cannot
    have me: they'll cremate
me in Sanskrit and sandalwood,
    have me sterilized
to a scatter of ash.

A.K. Ramanujan

                 Or abroad,
they'll lay me out in a funeral
        parlour, embalm me in pesticide,
bury me in a steel trap, lock
        me out of nature
till I'm oxidized by left
        over air, withered by my own
vapours into grin and bone.
        My tissue will never graft,
will never know newsprint,
        never grow in a culture,
or be mould and compost
        for jasmine, eggplant
and the unearthly perfection
        of municipal oranges.

Notes on the Poems

1. This poem, which echoes the style of the Soma Hymns of the Rig Veda, is AKR's own poetic adaptation of Wendy Doniger's translation of Rig Veda^8.79 published in her anthology of translations, *The Rig Veda: An Anthology of One Hundred and Eight Hymns* (Harmondsworth, Middlesex, England: Penguin Books, 1981), p. 121. The number in brackets after the title 'Soma' in fact refers to the page number in Doniger's book.
2. An earlier draft of this poem, titled 'Jazz Poem for Soma', was published in *Journeys* (2019), pp. 229–30.
3. 'Hindus speak of twenty-four senses' goes the first line in AKR's poem 'Twenty-Four Senses', published posthumously in Molly A. Daniels-Ramanujan's and Keith Harrison's (eds.), *Uncollected Poems and Prose: A.K. Ramanujan* (London and N. Delhi: Oxford University Press, 2001), p. 6.
4. Draft from 1979. Also titled 'Soma'. In an earlier version of this partially autobiographical poem 'this

man' is 'R.' See *Journeys*, p. 227–29. This poem is
inspired by mycologist R. Gordon Wasson's theory
that the ancient Soma was the mushroom *Amanita
muscaria*. R. Gordon Wasson, *Soma: Divine Mushroom
of Immortality* (The Hague: Mouton, 1968).

5. A Chicago newspaper.

6. A similar version of this poem was published in
Journeys, p. 225. AKR inserts here after the first
stanza his own translation of the ninth-century Tamil
saint Māṇikkavācakar from *Tiruvācakam*: IV.59–70
published in *Hymns for the Drowning* (1981), pp.
118–19.

7. Here AKR places below the first stanza this translation
from the tenth-century Tamil mystical poet Nammāḻvār
published in *Hymns for the Drowning*, p. 76.

8. Draft without a title. Dated 20 December 1980.
Published in *Journeys*, pp. 238–39.

9. Drafted in 1979.

10. Based on an early draft of 'Looking and Finding' (first
drafted 21 March 1971) published in *Second Sight*
(1986). Also titled 'He Looks and Finds'.

11. Drafted in 1972. The first stanza was published in
Journeys, p. 170. Several lines were incorporated in
'Looking and Finding', published in *Second Sight*.

12. Drafted in 1972. Published posthumously in *Journeys*,
p. 212.

13. Several earlier drafts of this poem are titled 'Soma: He
attends a conference' (dated 18 December 1974). A
later modified version was published as 'Some People'
in *Second Sight*, p. 72.

14. The first draft of this poem is dated 1976. Several drafts
of this unpublished poem are also titled 'Photographs
of War' until 1984.

15. Draft from the late 1970s. Other drafts from 1972 onwards are titled 'Soma: he suffers in the heat' and 'Sunstroke'.

16. Draft from the late 1970s. Sections of this poem were incorporated in 'Looking and Finding' published in *Second Sight*.

17. Draft from the late 1970s. Published in *Journeys*, p. 171.

18. Draft from the late 1970s.

19. Reference to Carlos Castaneda's *Journey to Ixtlan. The Lessons of Don Juan* (New York: Simon & Schuster, 1972).

20. Draft from 1979. There are several drafts from 1979 till 1984 with similar titles. Some lines resemble 'Poetry and our City' published posthumously in *The Black Hen* which appeared in *The Collected Poems* (1995), p. 242.

21. Draft from the early 1980s. Other versions also titled 'Soma: he looks at a rug' and 'A Chicken'.

22. A reference to the Soma sacrifice performed since Vedic times. Animals, such as goats or buffaloes, were sacrificed during the *agniṣomiya* ritual, for instance.

23. Drafted in 1979, this meta-poem refers to the linguistic and literary heritage of AKR and to contemporary Indian poets writing in English with whom he interacted, such as Nissim Ezekiel, Arun Kolatkar, Gieve Patel and R. Parthasarathy.

24. An earlier version of this poem, titled 'Soma: he reads a letter from his wife' (drafted in 1972) was published in *Journeys*, p. 170. The latest draft is titled 'He reads a letter from home' and elsewhere in the AKR Papers it appears as 'Extended Family I'.

25. This poem was published in *Second Sight*, p. 63, as 'Extended Family'. It was originally part II of a poem in two parts. 'Extended Family I' is published above (also titled 'He reads a letter from home').

26. AKR changed the title of this poem and published it as 'Death and the Good Citizen' in *Second Sight*, p. 25.

ADDITIONAL
FEATURES

The Post-Vedic History of the Soma Plant

Wendy Doniger

Preface
Mushrooms, India and Soma

In 1957, R. Gordon Wasson published his epoch-making book, *Mushrooms, Russia and History*. He continued to explore the world of mushrooms and psychedelic plants more generally, and eventually he stumbled on materials about the Soma plant in the Rig Veda, which the Vedic Indians had pressed to obtain from it a liquid that they drank and shared with the gods in their rituals. According to the Vedic texts, the Soma plant made them very high indeed, and it was also said to make them immortal.

In the early 1960s, Wasson wrote to Daniel H.H. Ingalls, the Wales Professor of Sanskrit at Harvard, asking him for help in exploring the possibly psychedelic nature of the Soma plant. Ingalls replied that he himself did not have time to take on this project, but that he did have a graduate student who might be willing to help. That was me, and that was the beginning of my collaboration and friendship with Gordon Wasson, which lasted until his death, in 1986.

As I worked my way through the Soma hymns of the Rig Veda, looking for possible clues to the botanical identity of the plant and sharing my discoveries with Gordon as I went along, he in turn educated me on the subject of psychedelic plants. At the same time, I was working on my Harvard PhD dissertation (1968) as well as on what would become my Oxford DPhil dissertation (1973). These projects involved, among many other things, the mythology of the god Indra, king of the gods, and one day I came upon a passage in the Mahabharata in which Indra was forced against his will to promise to offer the pressed Soma to a human Brahmin named Uttanka. As the Soma plant was said to make anyone who drank it immortal, Indra jealously guarded this privilege, and did not want to share it with Uttanka. Indra took the form of a low-caste naked hunter, appeared before the Brahmin, pissed a great stream right in front of him, and said, 'Drink it; it's the Soma.' The horrified Brahmin, of course, refused, thus inadvertently relinquishing forever his chance to drink the Soma and become immortal.

When I told this story to Gordon for his casual amusement, he astonished me by lighting up like a Christmas tree. 'The shamans!' he cried out, and he proceeded to tell me about the Siberians who drank the urine of shamans who had eaten the psychedelic mushrooms that they used to inspire their ritual trances. Could the story of Indra and the Brahmin perhaps allude to a similar tradition in the Vedas, and could Soma therefore be such a mushroom? Never mind that the Mahabharata story was composed many centuries after the Rig Veda; Gordon was determined to prove that Soma was a psychedelic mushroom.

And that was the genesis of the book that Gordon wrote with my help, *Soma: Divine Mushroom of Immortality*. He was an unlikely candidate for a druggie; he was a vice president at J.P. Morgan, a short, stocky man who dressed in conservative but elegant Brooks Brothers suits. We met often, sometimes in our flat in Cambridge, Massachusetts; sometimes in his apartment in the elegant Sutton Place in New York; sometimes in his beautiful home in Darien, Connecticut and, after 1965, in our flat in Oxford. It was long before the time of email, of course, but we exchanged letters and, occasionally, phone calls.

On the first occasion when I cooked for him, I prepared mushrooms in his honour and was disappointed to see that, as any idiot but me would have guessed, he was sick to death of mushrooms. But he ate them graciously, and, indeed, as I learned on further acquaintance with him, he ate anything he was offered. Once he told me of a visit he had made to Singapore, where he had been the guest of a group of wealthy Chinese bankers. They took him to a special restaurant and had ordered for him the pièce de résistance: two waiters carried out a large, live cobra, holding the snake taut between them; a third took a knife and cut out the heart and liver and offered them, still pulsating, to Gordon to eat; this was said to guarantee long life and virility.

'What did you do?' I asked Gordon.

'Of course I ate them,' he replied matter-of-factly. Clearly, he was not squeamish; I could well imagine him blithely eating whatever strange fruits he was offered during his botanical field work and travels.

As he read through the Soma hymns that I had translated for him, Gordon became more and more persuaded that the references to the shape of the plant, the way it swelled and was pressed, its colour, and other physical descriptions were persuasive evidence that it was indeed a mushroom, more particularly the red mushroom with white dots on it known as the fly agaric, *Amanita muscaria, Fliegenpilz, mukhomor, amanite tue-mouches*, and perhaps best known as the mushroom that gnomes sit on in many people's gardens. For my part, I felt that the Vedic descriptions were suggestive but not conclusive. Gordon, however, persuaded a number of important Indologists, among them my very own Daniel H.H. Ingalls and the great French Indologist Louis Renou, that the Soma plant was indeed *Amanita muscaria*.

In his drive to persuade a wider audience, Gordon was particularly determined to challenge the widespread misbelief that the mushroom was fatal. He was very cross with Dorothy Sayers, in one of whose murder mysteries (*The Documents in the Case*, 1930) someone is fatally poisoned by eating a brew of these mushrooms. In fact, people who eat the mushroom do often become quite ill; if the *idea* of drinking someone's urine does not make you ill, apparently you are less likely to get sick (and still able to get high) by drinking the urine of someone who has eaten the mushroom, as the nauseating poisons are filtered out in the passage through the intestines. But there is no record of anyone dying from eating the fly agaric mushroom. Gordon thought that mothers taught their children that they would die if they ate the mushroom because they didn't want their children to get high.

I myself soon became persuaded that Soma was certainly a psychedelic plant and perhaps a mushroom. I learned that the Soma plant was said to grow only above the timber line and hence became unavailable when the ancient Vedic Indians migrated down from the Himalayas into the Gangetic plain. I therefore believe that the various forms of yoga and other mind-altering praxes that arose in the Ganges Valley from the ninth to the sixth centuries BCE were inspired by the desire to recapture the ecstasy, the experience of *standing outside* one's own body and one's own mind, that had formerly been made possible by pressing and drinking the Soma plant. The importance of Gordon's discovery for our understanding of the history of religion in India is, therefore, very great indeed. I feel very lucky to have been even a small part of his extraordinary life and work.

Wendy Doniger
Chicago, October 2022

~

The history of the search for Soma is, properly, the history of Vedic studies in general, as the Soma sacrifice was the focal point of the Vedic religion. Indeed, if one accepts the point of view that the whole of Indian mystical practice from the *Upaniṣads* through the more mechanical methods of yoga is merely an attempt to recapture the vision granted by the Soma plant, then the nature of that vision—and of that plant—underlies the whole of Indian religion, and everything of a mystical nature within that religion is pertinent to the identity of the plant.

In place of such an all-inclusive study, the present essay attempts to summarize what has been written since Vedic times about the physical nature of the Soma plant and the substitutes for Soma. I have worked in the Bodleian Library and the Indian Institute at Oxford, the India Office in London, and the British Museum, and of necessity I have omitted the contributions of Indian scholars whose works are not available in those collections. Furthermore, I have dealt summarily with the Haoma of the Avesta, since the work done on the botanical identification of Haoma has been subsumed for the most part under the study of Soma.

I. The *Brāhmaṇas* and the *Srauta-Sūtras*

After the era of the Vedas there came a period when the centre of intellectual activity moved from the valley of the Indus to the upper Ganges and the Yamunā. A spate of works, the direct outgrowth of the Vedas and preserving ancient traditions, many of them lengthy, arose as a kind of corpus of ritual textbooks. These are the *Brāhmaṇas*, prose works dating from about 800 BCE.

Súrā is generally believed to have been an alcoholic drink of some sort—wine or rice wine or fermented liquor or beer or even distilled spirits[1]—or else to refer to alcoholic drinks in general. The *Brāhmaṇas* say clearly that Soma was not *súrā*. The *Śatapatha Brāhmaṇa* declares: 'Soma is truth, prosperity, light; and *súrā* untruth, misery, darkness.'[2] The *Taittirīya Brāhmaṇa* says, 'Soma is male and *súrā* is female; the two make a pair.'[3] The sharp distinction made by the text seems to rule out the possibility that Soma was simply another kind of alcoholic drink, and it would seem probable that *súrā* embraced all the fermented drinks that rated mention in the ṚgVeda.

The *Brāhmaṇas* are much preoccupied with the question of substitutes for Soma. They are books of ritual composed for the sacerdotal caste, and in places they seem to be deliberately obscure. If the priests knew what Soma was, they never stated it clearly, and their references to the Soma plant are ultimately of little help in establishing its botanical identity. It may be assumed that Soma was none of the plants expressly suggested as substitutes for it, though of course it may have resembled any of them in some particular and probably did so. But it is difficult to draw any sure conception from these negative hints, for the substitutes often bear little resemblance to each other, including as they do grasses, flowers, creepers and even trees.

The *Śatapatha Brāhmaṇa* sets forth an order in which substitutes should be used. First comes the reddish-brown (*aruṇá*) *phālguna* plant, which may be used because it is similar to Soma (*sómasya nyanga*), but the bright red (*lóhita*) *phālguna* plant must not be used. If *phālguna* is unavailable, then the *śyenahṛta* plant may serve, for there is a tradition that Soma was once carried away by a falcon, and a stalk (*aṃśú;*) fell from the sky and became the *śyenahṛta* plant. The third choice is the *ādāra* plant, which sprang from the liquor that flowed from the sacrificial animal when it was decapitated. Fourth comes the brown *dū́rvā* grass, which is similar to Soma, and the last choice is yellow *kúśa* grass. This being least satisfactory, a cow must be given in atonement.[4]

The *Tāṇḍya Brāhmaṇa* says that the *putīka* is the
plant which grew from a leaf (or feather, *parṇa*) that fell
when Soma was carried through the air, and that it is
therefore a suitable substitute.[5] In his commentary on
this work, Sāyaṇa says, 'If they cannot obtain the Soma
whose characteristics are described in the sacred text,
then they may use the species of creeper (*latā*) which is
known as *putīka*; if they cannot find *putīka*, then they
may use the dark grass (*śyāmalāni tṛṇāni*) known as
arjunāni.'[6] Yet another ætiological myth is used to explain
the substitution of the fruit of the *nyagrodha* (sacred fig
or banyan tree): the gods once tilted over their Soma
cups, and the *nyagrodha* tree grew from the spilt drops.[7]
Elsewhere it is said that even when Soma is available,
one should use the juice of the *nyagrodha* fruit for non-
Brahmans to drink.[8] It is probable that this fruit, like the
dūrvā and *kúśa* grasses, was accepted as a substitute for
Soma more by virtue of its own sacred nature than for any
resemblance to the Soma plant.

Various other substitutes for Soma appear in the
Brāhmaṇas: *syāmaka* (cultivated millet, said by the
Śatapatha Brāhmaṇa to be most like Soma of all the
plants),[9] *muñja* grass (sacred in itself), *kattṛṇa* (a fragrant
grass),[10] and *parṇa* (a sacred tree).[11] The European
lexicographers—Wilson, Roth, Monier–Williams—struggle
to identify all these plants in modern botanical terms
but often arrive at conflicting conclusions, as do the
Brāhmaṇas themselves. Certain pertinent facts emerge,
however, from the Brāhmaṇic literature:

1. The colour red is consistently associated with the
   Soma substitute. Red is the colour of the *nyagrodha*

flower; the colour of the *phālguna* plant;[12] the colour of the acceptable *dūrvā grass*;[13] and even the colour of the cow used in the purchase of Soma.[14]

2. There is a clear distinction between the identity of Soma and the identity of the substitutes. For Soma one must look to the ṚgVeda; for the substitutes, the *Brāhmaṇas* are the earliest sources of importance, but they contain no passages about the authentic Soma of sure evidential value. They are concerned with the ritual and symbolic nature of the Soma plant, not with its botanical identity.

II. Later Sanskrit Works

The writers of the post-Brāhmaṇic period, Sanskrit lexicographers and Vedic commentators, continued to dwell upon a multiplicity of plants that served as Soma, but most of them agreed upon only one thing: that Soma was a creeper (*vallī* or *latā)*. Yet nowhere in the ṚgVeda do these terms appear, Soma being there considered an herb (*óṣadhi*) or plant (*vīrúdh*). Amara Siṃha, the earliest of the Indian lexicographers (450 CE) gives many synonyms for what he calls *somavallī*, all of which Monier-Williams has the courage to define as *Cocculus cordifolius*. Amara also describes a plant that he calls *somarājī*, which Monier–Williams says is *Vernonia anthelmintica*.[15] These are distinguished from *súrā*.[16] The later lexicographers generally imitate Amara in their discussions of Soma: Medinī refers to an herb, the Soma creeper,[17] which Yāska had mentioned as an herb that caused exhilaration when pressed and mixed with water,[18] while Sāyaṇa, the most famous of the

Vedic commentators, refers to it as the Soma creeper.[19] Śabarasvāmi, another great commentator, also refers to Soma as a creeper, but one that yields milky juice;[20] this was to be retained as an acceptable attribute of Soma from then on through the European discussions, and the belief in the milky sap appears in the Hindu medical works as well.[21]

One might expect the early medical treatises to be less fanciful than the *Brāhmaṇas*, but this is not the case. The *Dhanvantarīyanighaṇṭu*, a medical work of 1400 CE, says that the Soma creeper yields the Soma milk and is dear to Brahmans.[22] The *Rājanighaṇṭu* describes the properties of Soma: the *somavallī* has great clusters and is a bow-like creeper, yielding the Soma milk; the *somavallī* is acrid, pungent, cool, black, sweet, and it serves to dispel biliousness, to quench thirst, to cause wounds to dry up, and to purify.[23] A more detailed, but hardly more scientific, description appears in the *Suśrutasaṃhitā*, a medical text in verse, dating from perhaps the fourth century CE, which reduces to its ultimate absurdity the passion for symmetry and classification that permeates these writings. It tells us that although there was originally created one kind of *somavallī*, it was then divided into twenty-four varieties: *aṃśuman* Soma smells like ghee; *muñjara* Soma has leaves like those of garlic; *garuḍahṛta* (= *śyenahṛta*) and *śvetākṣa* ('white-eyes') are pale, look like cast-off snake-skins, and are found pendant from the boughs of trees; etc.[24] Unfortunately, the enumeration of these varieties proves of limited value for botanical identification: one reads that all of them have the same qualities, all are creepers with milky juice, all are used in the same way, and all have fifteen black leaves, which appear one per day during the waxing moon and drop off one per day during the waning moon.[25]

Folk medicine and medical science in India are known collectively as *Āyurveda* ('The Sacred Knowledge of Long Life'). There is a widely quoted Āyurvedic verse, found both in Dhūrtasvāmi's commentary on Āpastamba's *Śrautasūtra* of the black Yajur Veda and in the *Bhāvaprakāśa*, that Max Müller cited in 1855 as the earliest 'scientific' description of Soma that he knew. It describes the plant as a black creeper, sour, leafless, yielding milk, having fleshy skin, causing or preventing phlegm, causing vomiting, and eaten by goats.[26] In spite of the admittedly late origin of this description, and in spite of the many equally authoritative descriptions in earlier Sanskrit works which contradict it, it served European scholars as a peg on which to hang their favourite theories. Its sharp detail and 'scientific' tone contrasted favourably with such descriptions as that of the *Suśruta,* and it seemed to agree with the descriptions of Soma given to Westerners by Indians of that day.

III. Early European References

The earliest non-Indian notices of Soma are in the Avesta, where the plant appears as Haoma, but these references are more obscure than those of the R̥gVeda; the question of the 'authenticity' of the Soma cult of the Avesta will be discussed below as it arises in the course of European discussions. The earlier parts of the Avesta—the *Yašts*—refer to Haoma as being strained for the sacrifice,[27] as the only drink which is attended with piety rather than with anger,[28] as a tall, golden plant[29] with golden eyes.[30] The

Yasna devotes three full hymns to Haoma (9–11), which it describes as growing in the mountains,[31] pressed twice a day,[32] odoriferous,[33] possessing many trunks, stems, and branches,[34] and yielding a yellow juice which is to be mixed with milk;[35] Haoma is golden and has a flexible stem.[36] The *Yasna* seems to distinguish between Haoma and other intoxicating beverages, of which it disapproves, but it has been suggested that Zoroaster hated the Haoma drinkers as well as drinkers in general.[37] Beyond this general description, and the evidence that the Soma cult was at least Indo–Iranian rather than simply Indian in its origin, the Avesta sheds little light on the Soma problem.

Megasthenes said of the Indians, 'They never drink wine except at sacrifices', distinguishing this sacrificial wine from their ordinary liquor—probably *súrā*—which he describes as 'composed of rice instead of barley'.[38] McCrindle suggests that this 'wine was probably Soma juice', and as the passage is certainly pre-Tantric it must in fact refer to Soma. Thus Megasthenes—misled no doubt by the similar rites among his own people—must be held responsible for the origination of a misconception that continues to plague Vedic studies to the present day. Plutarch speaks of a plant that the Iranians dedicated to a religious use:

> For pounding in a mortar an herb called ὄμωμι [ómomi] they invoke Hades and darkness; then having mingled it with the blood of a slaughtered wolf, they bear it forth into a sunless place and cast it away.[39]

Bernadakis conjectured that this ὄμωμι [ómomi] was the same as the μῶλυ [móly] of the *Odyssey* X 305, a fabulous herb probably cognate with the Sanskrit *mūla* (root); Orientalists of note, including Paul Anton de Lagarde,[40] have suggested that ὅμωμι [ómomi] was none other than the Haoma of the Iranians, the Soma of the Indians. In 1929, Emile Benveniste dismissed this notion:

> We must beware of correcting the text on this point, as the majority of editors have done following P. de Lagarde. The substitution of the plant μῶλυ [móly] for the enigmatic ὅμωμι [ómomi] is the device of harassed interpreters and is no better than the explanation of ὅμωμι [ómomi] by *hauma*; the first is arbitrary, and the second absurd . . . ὅμωμι [ómomi] is another name of *amomum* which is used in the cult of Ahriman as hauma is sacred to the cult of Ohrmazd.[41]

In 1771, A.H. Anquetil–Duperron brought out the first translation of the Avesta, after having spent some years in India in association with the Parsis. For the Haoma plant, he observed, the Parsis used a tree (*arbre*) which, they said, grew in Persia but not in India and resembled a vine but never bore any fruit. Anquetil–Duperron thought the plant resembled a kind of heather (*bruyère*), with knots very close together and leaves like those of jasmine. 'All these details lead me to believe that the *Hom* is the ἄμωμος [ámomos] of the Greeks and the *amomum* of the Romans.'[42] As the Indo–Iranian connection was not yet established, nor the Soma cult itself discovered, this suggestion was not pursued.

Then, in 1784, the first translation of a Sanskrit work into English appeared, Charles Wilkins's rendering of the *Bhagavad Gītā*. In it, he included a note: '*Sōm* is the name of a creeper, the juice of which is commanded to be drunk at the conclusion of a sacrifice.'[43] This is the earliest published citation of Soma in a European language that I have found. In his 1794 translation of the laws of Manu, Sir William Jones describes Soma as 'the moon plant (a species of mountain-rue)'.[44] H.T. Colebrooke then published his translation of the *Amarakośa*, saying that the *somrāj* was *Vernonia anthelmintica* (= *Conyza anthelmintica*),[45] but cautioning his readers that commentators seldom describe the plants they mention and that 'a source of error remains in the inaccuracy of the Commentators themselves . . . the correspondence of Sanscrit names with the generick and specifick names in Natural History is in many instances doubtful.'[46]

In 1814, William Carey published his *Hortus Bengalensis*, which was a summary of the manuscript that William Roxburgh was to publish in 1832. Carey identified *Sarcostemma brevistigma* (= *Asclepias acida, Sarcostemma acidum, Sarcostemma viminale, Cynanchium viminale*) as the plant known in Bengali and Sanskrit as *somalutā*, and also remarked that *Ruta graveolens*, a rue, bore the same Sanskrit name.[47] He did not link them with the Vedas, but he did take occasion to observe that Himalayan plants do not grow in Bengal,[48] an observation that was ignored by the Vedic scholars who later used Roxburgh's work to identify Soma.

In his 1819 *Sanskrit Dictionary*, Horace Hayman Wilson identified soma as 'the moon plant (*Asclepias acidum*) [= *Sarcostemma brevistigma*]', *somavallī* as 'a twining plant (*Menispermum glabrum*) [= *Tinospora cordifolia*]', or 'a medicinal plant (*Serratula anthelmintica*) [= *Vernonia anthelmintica*]'; in the 1832 edition of the dictionary, he added *somarājin*, which he defined as *Serratula anthelmintica*, though he still gave this as an alternative for *somavallī* as well.[49]

Sir Graves Chamney Haughton, in his 1825 edition of Jones's *Ordinances of Manu*, had corrected Jones's 'mountain rue' to 'swallow-wort (*Asclepias acidum*) [= *Sarcostemma brevistigma*]', probably following Carey. Finally, in 1832, William Roxburgh published his Flora Indica; he identified *Sarcostemma brevistigma* with *somalutā* in Sanskrit and Bengali, a plant (as he said) of much milky juice of a mild nature and acid taste. He added that 'native travellers often suck the tender shoots to allay their thirst.'[50] This is hardly the description of a plant that induces religious ecstasy, but Roxburgh identifies it with *sōm* mentioned by Wilkins as the sacrificial plant. He distinguishes it from *somrāj* (as Colebrooke had done in 1808), which is *Vernonia anthelmintica*, a plant with an acid taste,[51] and he further distinguishes *Calotropis gigantea* (= *Asclepias gigantea*) as the plant used by the natives for medical purposes.

From these beginnings down to our own time Soma has been identified with various species of Sarcostemma (= Asclepiads, related to the American milkweeds), of Ephedra, of Periploca, all of them leafless climbers superficially resembling each other, yet belonging to genera botanically far apart. Botanists in India would gather specimens, identify them with scientific names, and add the vernacular names that local helpers would give them, such as *somalutā*. Linguists and serious travellers would occasionally bring back plant names picked up in the various languages spoken from India to Iran that seemed to stem back to Soma or Haoma—e.g., *hum, huma, yehma; um, uma; um, umbur*[52]—and, linking them to the plant to which they belonged, present to the world another candidate for Soma. Most of these plants were or had been at some time used as substitutes for Soma or Haoma: to be eligible, plants had to meet certain requirements, which may have changed from area to area and from century to century. R.G. Wasson's Brahman informants said to him that the substitute 'Somas' had to be small, leafless, and with fleshy stems, attributes that are common in varying degrees to the three genera listed above and to the traditional descriptions in the *Brāhmaṇas* and medical texts.

IV. Mid-Nineteenth Century

For the next fifty years, Sanskritists and botanists alike merely elaborated upon Roxburgh's identification. Henry Piddington gives '*Sarcostemma viminale*' for the Bengali *soom* and '*Asclepias acidum*' for *somalutā*,[53] but these two names are now considered to represent the same species: *Sarcostemma brevistigma*. John Stevenson, in his translation of the *Sāma Veda*, says that Soma is '*Sarcostemma viminale*', 'the moon-plant' and describes in some detail the method of its use, observing that according to the commentator it is pressed and mixed with barley and allowed to stand for nine days, 'but how many days precede [the ceremony] and how many follow, I do not know . . . the Soma, when properly prepared, is a powerful spirit . . .'[54]

Vedic studies had now begun to assume considerable importance in Europe. In 1844, Eugène Burnouf published the first of a series of articles on Haoma, wherein he said that the Haoma juice, obtained by trituration, was the same as the Soma of the Vedic sacrifice, but he did not venture a botanical identification.[55] In 1845, J.O. Voigt published his *Hortus Suburbanus Calcuttensis*, a catalogue of the plants in the H.E.I.C. Botanical Garden. Once again *soma-rāj* is *Vernonia anthelmintica* and *shomluta* is *Sarcostemma brevistigma*; Voigt also mentions that farmers use the *Sarcostemma brevistigma* to rid their fields of white ants.[56] He draws attention to the use of the Asclepiads in general as emetics and to their acrid and bitter milk, and points out that in the West Indies they are a popular remedy for worms in children, given in doses of a teaspoon to a tablespoon.[57]

Friedrich Windischmann thought that the Soma plant might be *Sarcostemma brevistigma*, but he doubted that the Indian Soma was the same as the Haoma of the Persians, as the plant might have changed with the change in location. Yet he considered that the Avesta preserved the tradition of Soma and the sacrifice better than the ṚgVeda did, and he called attention to the Persian belief (remarked long ago by Anquetil–Duperron) that Soma did not grow in India.[58] Christian Lassen added his assent that Soma was *Sarcostemma brevistigma*,[59] and William Dwight Whitney wrote that Soma was:

a certain herb, the *Asclepias acida* [= *Sarcostemma brevistigma*], which grows abundantly upon the mountains of India and Persia . . . which, when fermented, possesses intoxicating qualities. In this circumstance, it is believed, lies the explanation of the whole matter. The simple-minded Arian [*sic*] people . . . had no sooner perceived that this liquid had power to . . . produce a temporary frenzy . . . than they found in it something divine . . .[60]

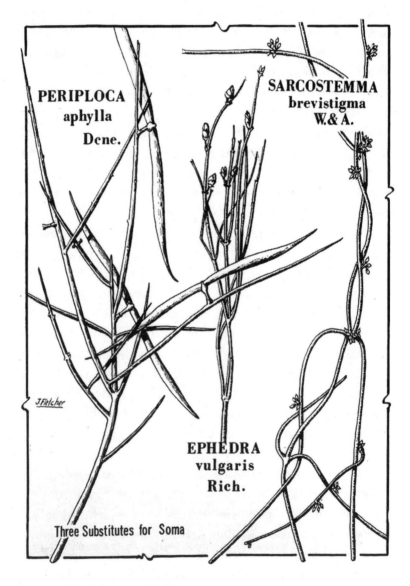

Fig. 1 Three substitutes for Soma.

Otto Böhtlingk and Rudolph von Roth accepted only tentatively *Sarcostemma brevistigma* as Soma, and perspicaciously added that it seemed to grow farther south than the Vedas indicate.[61]

Friedrich Max Müller in 1855 published an important article in which he quoted Dhūrtasvāmi's description of Soma[62] and said that this seemed to agree most strikingly with the accepted botanical descriptions of various Sarcostemmas. But he doubted whether the Vedic Soma would be found growing in Bombay (where the Sarcostemmas are found) rather than in the mountains of the North. Moreover, he asked, why would the Indians of the era of the *Brāhmaṇas* use *putīka* as a substitute for Soma if they could find 'Soma' itself—i.e., Sarcostemma spp.—right in Bombay?[63]

For thirty years no notice was taken of this Āyurvedic source, nor of Max Müller's doubts. Major Heber Drury accepted *Sarcostemma brevistigma* as *shom-luta*,[64] and Walter Elliot referred *somalatā* to the same species.[65] Martin Haug believed that the Persians had probably replaced the original Haoma with something else, retaining the name, and he thought that the present-day Soma of the Indians was in fact a substitute, but that the substitute retained in a measure the qualities of the true Vedic plant, with no leaves and a bitter white sap: 'It is a very nasty drink, but has some intoxicating effect,' he wrote, having tasted it several times but being unable to take more than a few teaspoonfuls.[66]

Sir George Christopher Birdwood, in his *Catalogue of the Vegetable Productions of the Presidency of Bombay, including a list of the drugs sold in the bazaars of Western India*, included *Sarcostemma brevistigma* under 'drugs', identifying it as the *somalutā* of the Vedas, a 'fermented liquor . . . mixed with barley and ghee . . . This wine was drunk at all their religious ceremonies and was used as an intoxicant by the rishis . . . Water passed through a bundle of *somalutā* and a bag of salt will extirpate white ants from a field watered with it.'[67] Birdwood identified *Sarcostemma brevistigma* with *S. acida* and expressed the view that 'the Som of the Vedas and the Hom of the Zend Avesta' were perhaps 'the real plant . . . present to the mind of the writer . . . of the first chapters of Genesis'[68]— an original contribution to the debate, and one of the few that is not echoed by anyone. In this year, Eugène Burnouf published his Sanskrit dictionary, wherein he described Soma as the juice of *Sarcostemma brevistigma*; the following year, J. Forbes Watson described the Soma plant as *Sarcostemma brevistigma*; the *somalatā* (Telegu) as the same species; and the *somalutā* (Sanskrit) as *Ruta graveolens*.[69]

Paul Anton de Lagarde (Paul Anton Boetticher) maintained that ὄμωμι [ómomi] was another word for μῶλυ [móly] or πήγανον [píganon], the mountain rue, and that it was a substitute used by the Greeks when they no longer had the *hōm* itself, the original sacred plant.[70] Drawing attention to the *Odyssey* verse describing the μῶλυ [móly] as a plant with a black root and a flower white as milk,[71] and to the mythological significance of rue,[72] Lagarde maintained that the description of the *harmal* (= *haoma* = ὄμωμι [ómomi] = μῶλυ [móly]) given by Arabian botanists described the plant precisely: a shrub with leaves like those of a willow and flowers like those of jasmine, with an intoxicating and soporific effect.[73] He added that Soma and Haoma were not the same plant, though they had the same name and use, and he linked the Soma of the ṚgVeda to rue by means of the Vedic epithet *sahásrapājas*, 'possessing a thousand *pājas*', which he related to the Greek term for rue, πήγανον [píganon].[74]

But no matter how many botanists and scholars accepted the Sarcostemma thesis, there were always reservations held in some quarters. In 1871, John Garrett declared flatly that 'the Soma of the Vedas is no longer known in India'.[75] Nevertheless, J.D. Hooker elaborated upon his earlier identification of Soma with *Sarcostemma brunonianum* by observing that this plant abounded in an acid milky juice and was 'hence eaten by the natives as salad, and sucked by travellers to allay thirst, thus forming a remarkable exception to the usually poisonous nature of the Asclepiadeous juices.'[76] Still there was room for new theories: Drury suggested that the 'moon creeper' might be *Calonyction muricatum (Ipomoea muricata)*, a plant whose swollen pedicels are cooked as vegetables and whose seeds are used as purgatives.[77] Nevertheless, Hermann Grassmann, whose Vedic dictionary is the standard work to this day, accepted the general view that Soma was a Sarcostemma.[78]

In 1873 Rajendra Lala Mitra revived the case for Soma as an alcoholic beverage. The original Indo–Aryans drank 'soma-beer and strong spirits,' which, when they moved to the hot climate of India, tended to make them ill. 'The later Vedas, accordingly, proposed a compromise, and leaving the rites intact, prohibited the use of spirits for the gratification of the senses.'[79] Soma was 'made with the expressed juice of a creeper (*Asclepias acida or Sarcostemma viminale*) [both = *Sarcostemma brevistigma*] diluted with water, mixed with barley

meal, clarified butter [ghee], and the meal of wild paddy
[*nīvāra*], and fermented in a jar for nine days . . . The
juice of the creeper is said to be of an acid taste, but I have
not heard that it has any narcotic property.' Mitra was
of the opinion that the starch of the two meals—barley
and wild paddy—produced 'vinous fermentation' and
that the Soma juice promoted fermentation and flavoured
the brew while checking the acetous decomposition, in
the manner of hops.[80] In this way, Mitra seemed to cover
every likelihood—except for the possibility that Soma was
not alcoholic at all but a plant containing a psychotropic
drug. It should also be pointed out that Mitra speaks
of 'soma-beer and strong spirits'. Presumably, he used
this latter term in its customary sense, meaning distilled
alcohol. This is an anachronism.

In 1874, Arthur Coke Burnell called attention to
the fact that there were different 'Somas' in different
parts of India, with the Hindus of the Coromandel coast
using *Sarcostemma brevistigma* in their rites and those
of the Malabar coast using *Ceropegia decaisneana* or *C.
elegans*.[81] In the following year, Martin Haug elaborated
on his previous descriptions by describing the Soma
plant as a small twining creeper with a row of leafless
shoots containing sour, milky sap; he identified the plant
as *Sarcostemma intermedium*, mentioning *S. brevistigma*
and *S. brunonianum* as related varieties and he expressed
his opinion that the plants denoted at the present time by
the terms *somalatā* and *somavallī* were later substitutes.[82]

In 1878, Friedrich Spiegel reported that the Indian
Parsis sent their priests to Kerman to obtain Haoma.[83] This
was the year that saw the publication of Abel Bergaigne's
La Religion Védique; Bergaigne thought that Soma was a

fermented drink and that milk was added to it to help the
fermentation process. He calls it a spirituous liquor, the
word spirituous (*une liqueur spiritueuse*) being applicable
in a broad sense to any volatile inebriating drink.[84]

In 1879, Heinrich Zimmer acknowledged that present-
day Hindus used a kind of Sarcostemma, citing Haug
and adding that the nausea Haug had experienced was
consistent with the *Brāhmaṇa* descriptions of Soma; but
he expressed doubts whether this plant, found in Bombay
and all over India, could have grown in the high sites of
Vedic civilization. He quoted various *Brāhmaṇa* references
to substitutes to support his thesis that Sarcostemma was
in fact just such a substitute, which had appeared in the
course of time.[85]

In 1881, Mitra reiterated his beer theory,[86] and
Kenneth Somerled Macdonald wrote. 'Soma is now
admitted, we believe, by the best Sanskrit scholars to
have been intoxicating. The numerous references in the
ṚgVeda are consistent only with such an interpretation.'[87]
He proceeded to repeat Mitra's theory in great detail,
though he failed to give Mitra credit for it.

The early 1880s saw the most enthusiastic and intense
period of the Soma debate. Scholarly tempers flared, new
and important names began to appear, and ingenious
theses were advanced. Rudolph von Roth began it with
an article in which he reviewed all the recent theories
about Soma as well as some of the *Brāhmaṇa* information;
he concluded that although *Sarcostemma brevistigma*
seemed to be well established as the present-day Soma
plant, there was no assurance that this plant—which grew
in the plains—was the Vedic plant, which must still grow
in the mountains.[88] Though he believed that the Soma

of the *Brāhmaṇas* was a substitute made necessary when the Vedic people moved away from their original home, he felt that the true Soma was probably some species of Sarcostemma or at least an Asclepiad, and he felt that any information about the present-day Soma might shed light on the Vedic plant.

In the following year, Edward William West expressed the opinion that the plants used for Soma in India and Persia at the present time were substitutes for the original Haoma–Soma plant, and he observed that the most common substitute in south and west India was the *Sarcostemma brevistigma*, 'a leafless bush of green succulent branches, growing upwards, with flowers like those of an onion', and resembling *Euphorbia tirucalli* or thornless milk-bush when not in flower.[89] In that same year, Angelo de Gubernatis, quoting Roth, expressed doubt whether the Soma plant could be identified at that time; he suggested that perhaps the Soma cult had shifted to wine in Persia, Asia Minor, and Greece, and that in India in later times its place was taken by a beverage offered to the gods and deliberately made unpalatable so that no mortal would be tempted to drink it.[90]

In 1883, Monier–Williams brought out his *Religious Thought and Life in India*. He defined Soma as *Sarcostemma brevistigma*, 'a kind of creeper with succulent, leafless stem', but he added, 'And yet it is remarkable that this sacred plant [the original, true Soma] has fallen into complete neglect in modern times. When I asked the Brahmans of North India to procure specimens of the true Soma for me, I was told that, in consequence of the present sinful condition of the world, the holy plant had ceased to grow on terrestrial soil, and was only to be found in heaven.' Nevertheless, a creeper 'said to be the true Soma' had been pointed out to him by Burnell in south India, where it was being used by orthodox Brahmans.[91]

In 1884, D.N. Ovsianiko–Kulikovskij published a book of some 240 pages devoted entirely to Soma and containing a great deal of learned and imaginative material; unfortunately, since it was published in Russian and never translated, it was not noted by subsequent scholars writing in other European languages, though Ovsianiko–Kulikovskij was familiar with all of the significant literature in German, French and English.[92] He maintained, on grounds of sound linguistic reasoning, that the word 'soma' applied first to the plant and later to the juice[93] and went on to discuss this plant:

> At the same time, the terms Soma and Haoma did not cease to signify also the divinity, whose gift or attribute the intoxicating beverage was considered to be. As concerns this last, it is presently obtained in India from a plant of the family *Asclepias acida*. Whether it was obtained from the same plant in antiquity, or from another, or if from another, from which particular one— all of these are questions that of necessity must remain for the time being without an answer. The description of the flower and the liquid of Soma in the RgVeda is not applicable to *Asclepias acida* and the beverage obtained from it.[94]

Ovsianiko–Kulikovskij described the sacrament of collecting Soma as taking place at night, 'in the light of the moon,' observing: 'Perhaps this feature has some link with the later identification of Soma with the moon.'[95] He continued:

> It was mixed with water, sour milk, and barley corn. Then it underwent fermentation, after which a strong, intoxicating beverage was obtained. The description of this procedure is met in a number of places in the ninth Maṇḍala of the ṚgVeda, but always in a fragmentary and often obscure form.[96]

This was the more or less conventional view of Soma, but then Ovsianiko–Kulikovskij went on to express his doubts that Soma had been a product of fermentation at all, and to suggest—in cautious but clear terms—that Soma might have been some sort of narcotic. This is by far the earliest reference to such a possibility, and it is significant that it appears in the writings of a Russian, who may have known of the Siberian cults:

> It is possible that the narcotic power of Soma was greater than the similar power of other drinks used in the time of the Veda; possibly it was of an essentially different nature. The action of Soma is always depicted in the most many-hued colours, as something fascinating, elevating, illuminating; on the other hand the action of common drink (*súrā*) is painted in far from such attractive colours . . . It is also quite possible that the superiority of Soma was entirely imaginary and rested solely on that religious sanction which fell to the portion of Soma (that is, not *Asclepias acida* or any other sort of Indian plant, but—Soma, as a religious and cultural psychological

conception) as early as the most remote Indo–Iranian antiquity.[97]

Roth then brought out another paper, in which he emphasized his feeling that Soma must still exist.[98] But he acknowledged that Albert Regel, the botanist employed by the Russian government, who had searched for Soma at Roth's request in the Syr Darya and Amu Darya watersheds, had reported finding no trace of a plant meeting Soma's description. Regel had expressed his opinion that the closest thing to Soma that he had found had been rhubarb, though he admitted that rhubarb was not used by the natives to make any intoxicating drink. Roth had supplied him with Vedic descriptions of Soma, and from them it was clear that none of the Asclepiads, Euphorbias, Ferulas, yellow Compositæ, or *Cannabis sativa* (hemp) conformed to the formula. Wilkens, a zoologist specializing in South Turkestan, had reported to Roth that in his opinion Soma might be *Peganum harmala*,[99] belonging to the Rutaceæ, though it lacked the sweetness and juiciness that the true Soma was thought to have had. Nothing daunted, Roth ended up with a flourish: 'Usbekistani today may drink their kumiss in cups in which Soma once gave them cheer . . . To find the Soma one need not be a botanist: the plant will have to be recognized in all its juiciness [*Saftfülle*] by every eye.'

V. File Number 118

Charles James Lyall, Secretary to the Chief Commissioner of Assam, translated Roth's papers and forwarded them, with his own remarks, to the Afghan Frontier Delimitation Commission. They in turn handed them over to the botanist George Watt, who published them with *his* added remarks under the heading, 'A note upon Dr Roth's suggestion regarding the Soma Plant', in a document issued as File No. 118 of the Government of India, Revenue and Agricultural Department, Simla, 20 August 1884.

Watt felt that Roth had produced no evidence that Soma was a species of Sarcostemma or any other Asclepiad; he considered it 'a great pity that Dr. Roth, instead of propounding his own theory at such length and in attempting to confute arguments against it, did not rather publish briefly the leading passages from Sanskrit literature descriptive of the plant . . . placing in the hands of the naturalist to the Commission a brief abstract from the Sanskrit authors, and thus leave his mind unbiased by any theories.' Watt was of the opinion that Soma was not necessarily a succulent, juicy plant but that it might be rather a dry branch used in a decoction, 'either by simple maceration or boiling.' He went on: 'Can any one who has examined the bitter milky sap of the Asclepiadæ . . . suppose that such a liquid could ever be used for more than a medicinal purpose, and still less become the Soma of the Vedas? It is much more likely that the oblong fruits of the Afghan grape, imported into the plains, as they are at the present day, afforded the sweet and refreshing cup of which our Aryan ancestors became drunk while wrapt in the oblivion of religious enthusiasm.'[100] He did not pursue this suggestion, however, and considered the Compositæ or Umbelliferæ more likely than the Asclepiads as candidates for Soma.

In reply to this, Max Müller wrote to the *Academy* journal on 20 October 1884, misquoting Haug ('it was extremely nasty and not at all exhilarating', where Haug had described the Soma he tasted as 'a very nasty drink, but [it] has some intoxicating effect'), referring to the *Brāhmaṇa* substitutes and the tradition that Soma 'was brought by barbarians from the North', and finally getting to the point—that he, Friedrich Max Müller, had published thirty years earlier the 'oldest scientific description of the Soma plant' that he knew of or had hope of finding, the Dhūrtasvāmi description of the dark creeper eaten by goats.[101]

On 9 November, Roth replied in the same journal to 'the learned scholar': 'I did not, indeed, remember the passage referred to; but if it had been in my mind I should scarcely have mentioned it . . .' He said it was impossible to date the '*Āyurveda*', that Max Müller's passage sounded like descriptions of 'the later, even the latest date, especially in the so-called *Nighaṇṭus*', taking exception to the adjective *vamanī* by insisting that 'it is not to be supposed that the Soma, or its principal substitute in later times, should have caused vomiting,' and, as a parting blow, correcting Max Müller's translation of *śleṣmalā* from 'destroying phlegm' to 'producing phlegm'. He concluded that the plant described was merely the 'Soma of later times which we know (that is, the *Sarcostemma acida* [*brevistigma*]), correctly described as bearing no leaves.' He still believed that the 'genuine original Soma' would bear great resemblance to its later substitute, and answered Watt's 'decoction' theory thus: 'I am sorry not to be able to conform my views to those of the distinguished botanist. The Aryans no more drank a decoction of the Soma plant than they drank tea or coffee. It would be, indeed, a disgrace to the interpreters of the Veda and Avesta if Dr. Watt were right.' He ended with the arch hope that the botanists of the Commission 'will not bring us home, as Soma, the Asafœtida, which there obtrudes itself upon one's notice, or any other Ferula.'

Max Müller replied on 17 November in another letter to the *Academy*, defending his Āyurvedic passage as the oldest *scientific* description of the Soma, standing up for his translation of *śleṣmalā* as dissolving rather than producing phlegm, and keeping his original reading for *vamanī* rather than the *pāvanī* (purifying) suggested by Roth. He admitted that 'this oldest scientific description of the Soma plant' might refer to a later substitute, and concluded: 'As to the Soma which the Brahmans knew (ṚgVeda X 85[3]), I shall welcome it whenever it is discovered, whether in the valley of the Oxus or in that of the Neckar.'

At this point the botanists entered the forum. J.G. Baker of the Kew Herbarium wrote to the *Academy* on 15 November, noting that Dr Aitchison had been selected as the botanist to attend the Afghan Delimitation Commission and supporting Max Müller's faith in the Sarcostemma, which, he pointed out, is eaten by men and animals throughout Sindh, Arabia, and Persia. He said that the flowers of the *Periploca aphylla* are eaten by the natives of Baluchistan 'and taste like raisins'. W.T. Thiselton–Dyer of the Royal Kew Gardens then supported Watt's suggestion of the Afghan grapes: 'That the primitive Soma was something not less detestable than anything that could be extracted from a Sarcostemma I find it hard to believe. When, however, the original Soma was unprocurable, and the use became purely ceremonial, the unpalatableness of the Soma substitute was immaterial.'[102] The Sarcostemma, according to Thiselton–Dyer, was chosen when the Soma plant was forgotten (or unavailable in the hot plains) because 'there is a faint resemblance in texture and appearance, though not in form, between the joint of a Sarcostemma and an unripe green grape', the Vedic Indians having had no word to distinguish a fruit from the stem of a plant, Thiselton–Dyer maintained.[103]

Max Müller answered this, on 8 December, with a reference to the Vedic tradition that Soma juice was mixed with barley milk, a process that, he suggested, was incompatible with the grape hypothesis but not with a kind of hops; he added that 'a venturesome etymologist might not shrink even from maintaining that hops and Soma are the same word,' deriving *hops* from Hungarian *komló*, mediæval Latin *humolo*, mediæval Greek χουμέλη [chouméli], and ultimately Sanskrit *soma*, 'which, for a foreign word, brought from Persia into Europe, is tolerably near . . . Now hops mixed with barley would give some kind of beer. Whether milk would improve the mixture I am not brewer enough to know.'

Charles G. Leland then wrote to the *Academy* to support the hops hypothesis with information about the *soma* or *sumer* ('the pronunciation is not fixed') of the Romany tongue, apologizing that 'any confirmation of this, drawn from such a very disreputable source as gypsy, is, indeed, not worth much', but pointing out that there was much Sanskrit in gypsy words and that *soma* in Romany meant 'scent or flavour . . . thus the hop gives the *suma* or *soma* to the beer, as the lemon to punch.' He added that the fact that hops do not grow in the present dwelling place of the Hindus confirms rather than disproves Max Müller's theory, since if it were still available there the Indians would be using it instead of the present substitute. At this point (20 December), A. Houtum–Schindler wrote from Teheran with a tale of a Sarcostemma that he had been shown by the Parsis in Kerman, a plant with a greenish white juice and a sweetish taste that caused vomiting when taken in amounts of more than a dozen drops, and that corresponded closely with Max Müller's Āyurvedic description—*if* it was viewed only 'several days after it had been collected', by which time the stalk would have turned dark, the juice turned sour, and the leaves fallen off. To this ingenious postulate, he added several descriptions of the *Hum* plant from various Persian dictionaries, including one of a deadly poison the fruit of which is much liked by partridges and which resembles a tamarisk tree—'the latter qualities evidently refer to another plant'. W.T. Thiselton–Dyer then identified still another plant used by the Parsis in their rites—the *Ephedra vulgaris*, which, he said, bore sweet red berries and somewhat resembled *Tamarix articulata*, like the plant mentioned by Houtum–Schindler: 'But he [Houtum–Schindler] also says it is "a deadly poison" (though apparently not to partridges). This does not agree with Ephedra, which is browsed by goats.'

On this note, the *Academy* correspondence ended, but the argument continued. On 25 January 1885, Watt published his 'Second Note on the Soma Plant', in which he said that a Dr Dymock of Bombay had sent him a Haoma plant, which was *Periploca aphylla* and had told him he thought that the plant was not used to obtain liquor but that a small portion of it was added to a liquor obtained from grain; he added that, according to the Parsis, the Haoma never decayed. This strengthened Watt's opinion that Soma was not a succulent plant, certainly not a Sarcostemma, an opinion that was further encouraged by a letter he had received from Rajendra Lala Mitra, who had suggested that Soma might have been used like hops as an ingredient in the preparation of a kind of beer and that the Vedic phrase 'Soma juice' was merely a figure of speech. 'The word "sweet",' Mitra wrote, 'which has so much puzzled the learned Professor von Roth, may be safely, nay appropriately, used in a poem in praise of bitter beer.' Watt was therefore convinced that the Haoma plant was the Soma after all and that 'the dry and bitter twigs' had been used to flavour some other beverages, 'much in the same way as Acacia bark is used throughout India'. In passing, Watt rejected a suggestion he had received from Benjamin Lewis Rice that Soma might have been 'sugarcane or some species of sorghum'. He concluded that *Periploca aphylla*—the Haoma of Dr Dymock— was after all the most likely Soma plant, and he quoted Baker's description of *Periploca aphylla* as having 'flowers fragrant, eaten by natives, taste like raisins'.

Surgeon General Edward Balfour, in the third edition of his *Cyclopædia of India*, maintained that the Soma of Vedic times was a 'distilled alcoholic fluid' made from *Sarcostemma brevistigma*, which flowers during the rains in the Deccan. In the same article, he referred to the Soma juice as 'a fermented liquor' and 'this beer or wine'; he believed that this liquid was used at all religious festivals and by the rishis at their meals; and he attributed to Windischmann the suggestion that the Soma plant may have been the gogard tree.[104]

In 1885, Julius Eggeling published the second volume
of his translation of the *Śatapatha Brāhmaṇa*, wherein he
observed that the exact identity of the Soma plant was 'still
somewhat doubtful', but that every probability seemed to
favour *Sarcostemma brevistigma* or some other plant of
the same genus. In answer to Watt's suggestion that the
opinions of all the 'Sanskrit authors' be assembled for
the botanists to use, Eggeling wrote: 'One might as well
ask a Hebrew scholar to give accurate descriptions of the
"lily of the valley" to enable the botanist to identify and
classify the lovely flower which delighted the heart of King
Solomon. It is exactly the want of an accurate knowledge
of the nature of the Soma plant which prevents Vedic
scholars from being able to understand some of the few
material allusions to it.'[105] Undaunted, Aitchison wrote
a letter to the Daily News (13 March 1885) expressing
his opinion that Soma was wine after all. He modified
this, however, when he returned from Afghanistan
and published *The Botany of the Afghan Delimitation
Commission*, wherein he informed his readers that the
natives of North Baluchistan call *Periploca aphylla*,
Ephedra pachyclada, and another *Ephedra 'Hum, Huma,
and Yehma'*. He said that the natives eat the small red
fruit of these plants, but he hesitated to identify any of
them with the original Soma.[106] Finally, in 1888, Max
Müller republished the *Academy* correspondence in his
Biographies of Words and the Home of the Aryans[107] with
additional notes by Thiselton–Dyer, who supported Max
Müller by saying that Soma 'was certainly in later times
a fermented drink made from grain, to which the Soma
plant itself was only added as an ingredient.' Observing
that, according to Roxburgh, the Sarcostemma was

'not necessarily nauseous', he nevertheless rejected it
as a possibility for the Primitive Soma, rejecting as
well Houtum–Schindler's *Hum* (which he identified as
Periploca aphylla) and his tamarisk-like plant (which he
identified as *Periploca hydaspidis*, indistinguishable, he
said, from *Ephedra foliata* except when in flower). He
concluded with the belief that the Sarcostemma was used,
like hops, to flavour the 'more effective ingredients' of
fermented grain and that it was used *not* 'as a ceremonial
reminiscence of the grape but in the absence of the
original Soma plant—the hop. George Watt concluded
this episode with his article on Ephedra in the *Dictionary
of the Economic Products of India*, where he rejected,
among other hypotheses, his own former suggestion of
the Afghan grape, though he could not resist noting that
wild grapes are called '*Um, Umbur*' in Kashmir.[108] He
mentioned that *Ephedra vulgaris* grew in the Himalayas,
that *Ephedra pachyclada* and *E. foliata* were found in
Garhwal and Afghanistan, that *Periploca aphylla* was
used sometimes in Bombay, but that the Parsis' *huma*
was usually an Ephedra. He said that *putīkas* (Basella
spp.), when stripped of their leaves, would resemble
Sarcostemmas; that *Vernonia anthelmintica* and
Pæderia fœtida are known as *somaraj* in Hindustan; that
Asclepiads are emetics and are eaten by goats; and that
Sarcostemma is rare but Periploca plentiful in Central
Asia. He rejected the Periploca, however, on the grounds
that the Aryans would have recognized it in India and not
used the Sarcostemma in its place. And from all this, he
concluded that Soma refers to 'an early discovery of the
art of fermentation' rather than to any plant in particular.
All the sound and fury had proved nothing, after all.

VI. The Turn of the Century

Still the battle raged, if more quietly, over the same ground. Adalbert Kuhn said that Haoma and Soma were separate plants resembling each other in name and external appearance, the Soma of present-day India being *Sarcostemma brevistigma* (an identification that he chose to attribute to Roth), which was not however the original or at least the only plant from which Soma was taken.[109] John Firminger Duthie then added an odd piece of information that went unnoticed: The Marwara people call the spiked grass known as *Setaria glauca* Soma.[110] Darmesteter in his translation of the Avesta referred to Haoma as a yellow plant with very close-set knots[111] 'like the Indian Soma'.[112] Monier-Williams' dictionary (1891) simply gave *Sarcostemma brevistigma* for Soma, and J. Börnmuller mentioned that he had met with a Parsi priest in Yezd carrying *huma*.[113] At once he recognized it as *Ephedra distachya*, and thus he had solved at last the problem mentioned to him first by Max Müller in Oxford. He added that the plant grew all over Central Asia and that large quantities of it were dried and sent from Persia to Bombay every year.

Alfred Hillebrandt then produced his extensive summary of the recent Soma theories and introduced his own famous theory that Soma was the moon throughout the ṚgVeda. He explained that contemporary Soma plants were probably not the same as the original, that substitutes had been used as soon as the Aryans left their homeland in the Sindh, and that the Vedas themselves were self-contradictory, since they had been compiled in various times and places.[114] He pointed out that Soma

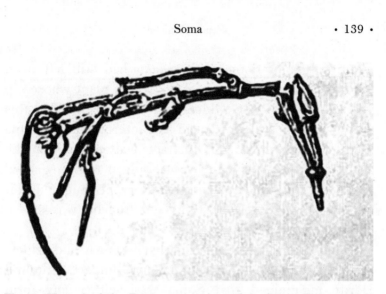

Fig. 2 'Haoma' of the Persians. As pictured in James Darmesteter's translation of the Avesta, 1890–1892. Said to be life-size.

was not a blossoming plant and therefore could not be hops as Max Müller had suggested; that Soma had a red stalk and reddish brown sap; and that the epithet 'with hanging branches' (naicāśākhá)[115] probably referred to the nyagrodha (Ficus religiosa), which was an important substitute. In fact, he concluded, even at the time of the RgVeda itself, various plants were already in use, and he cited Burnell's evidence that different Somas were used simultaneously in different parts of India.

Hermann Oldenberg devised a new theory, suggesting that the original Soma was itself a substitute, not for wine but for the Indo–European honey drink, mead or hydromel.[116] Of course it had long been recognized that the Sanskrit mádhu, the Greek μεθυ [methy], and English mead were cognate, and that mádhu was applied to Soma in the RgVeda (whence all the trouble over the bitterness of Sarcostemma), but mádhu was a general term applied to milk and rain as well as to Soma, and the simple identification of Soma with *mádhu* had still left open the botanical identification of Soma as a plant whose sap was known as honey. Oldenberg, however, avoided this difficulty by postulating mead as a forerunner and Soma as a later substitute: this distracted attention from the Soma plant itself (since it was no longer to be regarded as the *original*, the Ur-plant, that everyone sought) but it did not, of course, add anything at all to what was known about the Indian Soma.

This theory was to become well-known and widely accepted, but it had little immediate impact. Edmund Hardy maintained that Soma was neither any form of honey nor súrā but most probably *Sarcostemma brevistigma* after all.[117] Vedic scholars generally clung to the Asclepiad hypothesis[118] or they hazarded even less: P. Regnaud called Soma 'une liqueur enivrante', and cautioned against taking the Vedic texts literally when they spoke metaphorically.[119] Rustomjee Naserwanyil Khory covered some *very* old ground by considering a *Brāhmaṇa* substitute to be the original Soma;[120] he identified Soma (*somavallī* in Sanskrit, *amṛtavallī* in Bengali) as a climbing shrub called *Tinospora cordifolia*, the extract of which (called *gurjo, gilo*, etc.) is used as an aphrodisiac, a cure for gonorrhea and a treatment for urinary diseases. Christian Bartholomæ in his famous *Altiranisches Wörterbuch* (1904) described Haoma as a plant used in medicine, for magic, and as an alcoholic drink, but he refrained from identifying the plant. W.W. Wilson thought Soma was the σιλφιον [silfion] (Latin *laserpitium*) mentioned in a fragment of Alcman as a plant that has wonderful properties, grows on mountains, is golden, and is plucked by birds.[121] He supported this

argument with complex Indo–European linguistics but
was cautious enough to note: 'It is not improbable that
even at the time of the Vedas, use was made of more
than one kind of plant. W. Caland and Victor Henry
considered the question of the identification of Soma
insoluble.[122] Henry maintained that the Indo–Aryans
had imported Soma ever since they entered the area of
northwest India, and that the present-day Soma of India
did not correspond to the Vedic descriptions of its taste or
characteristics.[123] Still, the old definitions persisted: K.L.
Bhishagratna in his 1907 edition of the *Suśruta* defined
somalatā as *Sarcostemma brevistigma* and *somarājī* as
Vernonia anthelmintica. Maurice Bloomfield referred
to Soma merely as 'an intoxicating drink . . . regarded
as the tipple of the gods',[124] and A.A. Macdonell and
A.B. Keith concluded that the RgVeda descriptions
were 'inadequate to identify the plant . . . It is very
probable that the plant cannot now be identified.'[125] Then
Hermann Brunnhofer came forward to defend Lagarde's
'mountain rue' (originally Sir William Jones's theory,
though Lagarde did not say so and probably did not
know of Jones's opinion). Brunnhofer maintained that
Lagarde had already solved the Soma question forty years
previously, 'though the Vedists still ignore him.'[126] He
elaborated upon Lagarde's theory by mentioning Pliny's
description of a plant known as ἀμβροσία [ámvrosía]
possessing characteristics that suggested a kind of rue to
Brunnhofer.[127] He then called attention to the RgVedic
verse (IV 3[9c]), perhaps an oblique reference to Soma,
that speaks of a black cow giving white milk; Brunnhofer
considered this a perfect description of the μῶλυ [móly], a
dark plant with white milk.

In 1911, Carl Hartwich published *Die menschlichen Genussmittel*, in which he discussed various forms of tobacco, alcohol, and drugs.[128] He included 'Soma–Haoma' in his study, but was uneasy about its status as a drug or stimulant ('*Genussmittel*'); having described various accepted botanical 'Somas' (*Sarcostemma brevistigma, Periploca aphylla, Basella cordifolia*, etc.), he went on to say: 'Although all of these have been tested—though not altogether thoroughly—none of them is known to have stimulating or sedative or other characteristics which could mark it as a drug or stimulant.' He therefore considered it possible that they might have been used as supplements, perhaps as spices, to the other known ingredients of the Soma drink (meal, milk, and whey) in which alcohol might have been produced.[129] The possibility that Soma might have been some other plant that did have 'stimulating or sedative characteristics' does not seem to have occurred to him, though he granted that the Persians used for their Haoma a different plant (*Ephedra vulgaris*) containing a drug (ephedrine) which caused dilation of the pupil.[130] One of the plants that Hartwich gave as an alleged Soma was *Vitex negundo*, whose bitter leaves and root were used against fever. Since the plant was originally native to tropical America, Hartwich dismissed it as a possible Soma, but observed in conclusion that in India it was known as *Indrahasta* and *Indrasurā* ('the hand of Indra' and 'the wine of Indra').[131] It may be that this association with Indra—together with Indra's fondness for Soma (to which Hartwich refers)— recommended the *Vitex negundo* to Hartwich, for he gives no Sanskrit names for any of the other plants he mentions. Yet in this context it is surprising that he did not mention

Indrāśana ('the food of Indra')[132] which was a common name for hemp, *Cannabis sativa*, the leaves of which were dried and chewed, supplying just the *Genussmittel* that Hartwich seemed to seek.

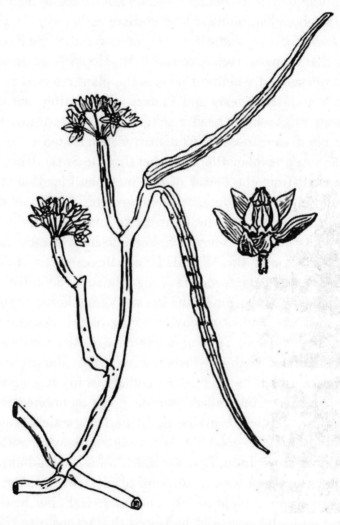

Fig. 3 'Soma'. As pictured in Zenaīde A. Ragozin: Vedic India, New York, 1895.

Keith reassembled the old evidence but still considered the Soma problem insoluble,[133] and L.H. Mills produced an odd throwback in which he insisted that Haoma and Soma grew independently from the same original, and that 'nothing humorous, let us remember, attached to the idea of [alcoholic] stimulus at first in those early days'.[134] The *Oxford History of India*[135] merely observed that the Parsis say that Soma is Asclepias, and E.W. Hopkins concurred but questioned whether this was the plant referred to in the Vedas, the Avesta and Plutarch, suggesting that the names might have been retained when substitutes for the plant were used.[136] Chapman Cohen stated without reference or explanation his belief that the Soma drink 'is prepared from the flower of the lotus', an idea that was bound to occur to someone sooner or later, in view of the *Odyssey* tradition of the lotus-eaters and the sanctity of the lotus in India, but which seems to have attracted no supporters after this.[137] E.B. Havell then suggested that Soma was *Eleusine coracana* or *rāgi*, the common millet, an idea that he supported on the basis of Vedic characteristics (shaped like udders, tawny, growing in the mountains) and the *Śatapatha Brāhmaṇa* reference to *dūrvā* and *kuśa* as substitutes, both of which resemble *rāgi*, 'the common millet still used in the Eastern Himalayas for making the intoxicating drink called *Marua*.'[138] He mentioned that the Brahmans, while preparing Soma, 'sang a song which reminds one of a good old Aryan sailors' chantey, with a refrain, "Flow, Indu, flow for Indra".'[139] Havell admitted that, 'whether fermentation took place before or after it was so used is a point which is not very clear', but he was clear on its history: *rāgi* had been the Aryans' principal food and drink until they moved to the Ganges Valley

and switched to rice, 'and, perhaps under the influence
of Buddhism, gradually gave up intoxicating liquors,
or "went dry".' Then they used substitutes for the *rāgi-
Soma*, forgot its name and retained contact with it only as
the food of the lowest caste, the Śūdras. Havell said that
Marua when kept too long is nauseating and evil-smelling,
in keeping with certain descriptions of Soma, but when
fresh 'it is an exhilarating drink that easily intoxicates the
uninitiated.' He then administered the coup-de-grâce: the
Indo–European myth of the bringing of Soma from heaven
by an eagle is explained by the simple fact that birds lined
their nests with *rāgi*. One would hardly think that this
argument merited rebuttal, but it did in fact stimulate an
answer that was to become the last significant theory of
Soma: Mukherjee's theory that Soma was hemp, *Cannabis
sativa* (= *Cannabis indica*), known to the initiate as *bhang*
(the Hindi term derived from Sanskrit *bhaṅgá*, m., or
bhaṅgā, f.), ganja, hashish, marijuana or pot.

VII. Mukherjee and the Bhang Theory

Braja Lai Mukherjee[140] picked unlikely grounds on which
to challenge Havell's flimsy theory, which he said was
based upon considerations 'which may be supplemented
by others of a more important character', e.g., that there
was no reference to cows' udders in the ṚgVeda.[141] He
then supplied an elaborate 25-point argument to show
that Soma was in fact not *Eleusine coracana* but *bhang*:
Śatapatha Brāhmaṇa 5.1.1.12 says that Soma is *uśānā*;[142]
Soma was 'originally amongst the Kirātas', a mountain
tribe; amongst the Kirātas, *u* and *a* were articular prefixes;
therefore *uśānā* = *śaṇa*; *śaṇa* is hemp; the Tanguts call

hemp by the name *dschoma*; hemp = Greek *kanna* [*sic*] = Sanskrit *śana*; the Tibetan word for hemp is *somaratsa*; the preparation of Soma is similar to that of *bhang*; the deity Mahādeva (Śiva) is a lover of *bhang*; *bhang* is used by the modern representatives of the Vedic people in the celebration of worship of the goddess Durgā, which is a Soma sacrifice.[143] The final link in the argument is this: '*Bhang* is sacred to Hindus by tradition.' In sum, 'May we not conclude that the weight of evidence is in favour of the identification of Soma with *Cannabis (bhang)*?' This strange argument, combining linguistic reasoning with the purest twaddle, was further developed by Mukherjee in his book, *The Soma Plant*,[144] which was reviewed in a brief paragraph by L.D. Barnett, who said blandly that Mukherjee made out a good but not always convincing case for hemp as Soma.[145]

Sir Charles Eliot expressed 'considerable doubt' that Soma could be identified. He said it was a plant with 'yellow juice of a strong smell, fiery taste, and intoxicating properties', and that the Parsis of Yezd and Kerman used Asclepiads.[146] N.B. Pavgee rebutted Havell without proposing any alternative, using the argument merely as a foil for his own hypothesis—that Soma was indigenous to the Saptasindhu region (i.e., India proper) and was not 'brought in' by 'Aryans.' The Indo–Aryans were autochthonous in India, he wrote, and 'had not immigrated'; the Iranian Soma is, of course, spurious, but kept the old name. Soma could not be any kind of liquor, for liquor is an evil, while Soma—the true Soma—was 'exhilarating yet slightly intoxicating' and 'gave moral elevation'. Pavgee does not explain how this was done, nor does he identify the Soma plant.[147]

In 1922, Jakob Wilhelm Hauer published a work
that lent a kind of peripheral support to the *bhang*
theory, for he referred to the Soma cult as the most
highly developed form of the use of narcotics to induce
ecstasy, calling particular attention to the late Vedic hymn
(X 136) that describes a long-haired sage who drinks
poison with Rudra.[148] Hauer believed that Soma was the
most important toxic means of inducing ecstasy, but not
the only such means, and he suggested that the Vedic
references might be traces of a primitive ecstatic practice
of hallucination caused by certain plants.[149] Whether
these 'plants' were Sarcostemmas, Afghan grapes or
hemp, Hauer neglects to say, but his final remark is more
suggestive of a hallucinogenic plant than of anything
else: opium is no longer used in a religious context, but
every time we light up a good cigar we experience a faint
reflection of the splendour of the rapture of the primeval
ecstatic.[150] Though this ancient Yogic cult is clearly non-
Vedic, presumably pre-Vedic, Hauer does not say whether
he believes the Soma plant to have been the same as the
drug of the 'primeval ecstatic', or perhaps a substitute for
it. Yet his remarks are provocative in the context of the
search for a hallucinogenic Soma plant.

VIII. Later Researches in the Twentieth Century

In 1924, Gilbert Slater advanced a novel hypothesis:
that *amṛta* (Soma) was Egyptian beer, a fermentation
of date juice or palmyra palm or coconut palm, brought
to India from Mesopotamia.[151] This theory was noted
but not accepted. Georges Dumézil maintained that
Soma was native to India, and that it was the Indian

substitute for the Indo–European 'sacred barley beer' rather than for the Indo–European mead that Oldenberg had postulated.[152] The beer was replaced by wine in Greece and by Soma in India, and the one word for this beer, or for a beverage with a cereal base which must have preceded it, was the sacred ritual name: ambrosia, the Greek ἀμβροσία [ámvrosía] and the Sanskrit *amṛta*, the elixir of immortality. Barley itself must have been Indo–European, as the linguistic evidence indicates: Greek χριϑή [chrithí], Latin *hordeum*, Armenian *gari*, and various Celtic words for beer, e.g., *cervesia* (Gallic) and *cuirm* (Irish). As for the sacred position of barley in India, Dumézil referred to the tradition that barley (*yava*) had stayed with the gods when all the other plants had left them, thus enabling the gods to conquer their enemies.[153] The *Mahābhārata* relates that the gods once churned the ocean in order to obtain the *amṛta*, but a terrible poison emerged and would have destroyed them all had Śiva not swallowed it and saved them; in the light of Dumézil's theory that the *amṛta* is barley beer, this myth is an expression of excessive fermentation that must be arrested.[154]

Louis Lewin's *Phantastica: Narcotic and Stimulating Drugs* included Soma in the chapter on alcohol rather than narcotics, mentioning *Periploca aphylla, Sarcostemma brevistigma, Setaria glauca,* and *Ephedra vulgaris* as plants that had been identified with Soma, but he added: 'None of these plants is able to give rise to such effects as have been attributed to Soma . . . I regard Soma as a very strong alcoholic beverage obtained by fermentation of a plant.'[155] Elsewhere, he suggested that the yogis might have used some sort of narcotic, such as Indian hemp or scopolamine, but he did not identify this practice with the cult of Soma.[156]

The Sarcostemma theory returned yet again, this time in a paper by L.L. Uhl, who maintained that Sarcostemma, and not Ephedra, was the original Soma, saying that he had found *Sarcostemma brevistigma* frequently at latitude 15° in south India, where it is called Soma and is used in sacrifices.[157] Arthur Berriedale Keith expressed the view that the Soma problem, though insoluble, had led to 'interesting investigations, but to no sure result, and the only thing certain is that the plant, which has been used in modern India as the Soma plant, is one which would not be considered by modern tastes as at all pleasant in the form of pressed juice mixed with water.'[158] Then, somewhat echoing de Gubernatis' reasoning, Keith went on to say that although one can't be sure what was pleasant to a Vedic Indian, nevertheless it is likely that 'the drink was originally a pleasant one; in the course of time the long distance from which the shoots had to be brought may easily have made it less attractive, as it certainly encouraged the use of various substitutes described in the ritual text books.' Keith agreed with Hauer's suggestion that ṚgVeda X 136 might be a reference to the use 'of some poison to produce exhilaration or hypnosis',[159] relating this to a verse about hemp (*śaṇa*) in the *Atharvaveda*,[160] but not to Soma. Elsewhere he observed that the Avesta does not call Haoma mead, and suggested that mead was the Indo–European drink and that Soma was identified with it when Soma was discovered, in India, and found to produce 'a juice pleasant to drink or at least intoxicating'.[161]

In 1926, G. Jouveau-Dubreuil wrote an article suggesting that Soma was none other than a species of Asclepias after all.[162] He had discovered that the Nambudri Brahmans (on the Malabar coast, in Kerala) of Taliparamba, who practised 'pure Vedic ceremonies', sent to a Raja in Kollangod at the foot of the high mountains to obtain their Soma plant, a leafless, milky, green creeper that was an Asclepiad. *Plus ça change . . .* Yet neither the Sarcostemma theory nor the theory that Sarcostemma was merely a substitute was incompatible with the beer theory of Max Müller and Mitra (for the beer could be made with the Sarcostemma or the plant for which it was a substitute), nor were these or the wine theory incompatible with Oldenberg's mead theory (for the mead could have been replaced by any of the above in India), and so the theories continued to live side by side. Otto Schrader and A. Nehring maintained that the Indo–European honey was replaced by the Soma plant—still called *mádhu*—in Aryan times, while wine and beer were later substituted for it throughout Europe.[163] P.V. Kane was unconvinced by any of the theories, but mentioned that in the Deccan a plant called *rānsera* was used as a substitute for Soma.[164]

In 1931, Sir Aurel Stein published a paper entitled, 'On the Ephedra, the Hum Plant, and the Soma',[165] describing a cemetery in Central Asia filled with packets of Ephedra twigs. Recalling the evidence for Ephedra as Haoma and Soma and quoting Wellcome's *Excerpta Therapeutica* for evidence that the Chinese use an Ephedra called *Ma-huang* to get an alkaloid drug (ephedrine), he then followed this with the assertion that Ephedra could not have been the original Soma, for it was bitter and Soma sweet, and Ephedra was not mountainous. He then concluded: 'The only result of these inquiries has been to direct my attention more closely to . . . the wild rhubarb', which grows in the mountains, has a fleshy stalk, and can be made into rhubarb wine, though Stein admits that the Indians do not do so.[166] Granting that the Vedic descriptions of the Soma plant could apply to Asclepias or rhubarb—or to anything else, for that matter—Stein nevertheless maintained that the descriptions of the Soma *juice* best applied to rhubarb. He added that the juice might be mixed with milk to facilitate fermentation, 'which alone could endow a juice like that obtained from the rhubarb with the exhilarating and exciting effect so clearly indicated in the Vedic hymns.'[167]

Perhaps the strangest episode in the history of Soma research came in 1933, with a truly Twentieth Century theory of Soma. Dr Paul Lindner of Berlin published an article entitled, 'The Secret of Soma'.[168] He referred to a statement by E. Hubers that Soma was merely a decoction of barley or millet, into which the juice of the Soma plant had been added as a catalyst for fermentation (*Gärungserreger*), though it was unclear what kind of fermentation took place.[169] Lindner's own studies of the micro-organisms of the Agave in Mexico, particularly of *Thermobacterium mobile*, had brought him to the conclusion that yeast played only a secondary role in the fermentation, after the fermentation-bacteria had prepared the field. He went on to say that *Thermobacterium mobile* can produce alcohol in grapes and in cane sugar, and concluded that since the 'purity of fermentation' took precedence over the material fermented, even *Sarcostemma brevistigma, Calotropis gigantea*, or *Ephedra distachya*, which had been considered as 'the holy Soma plant', might have yielded the juice 'which was enjoyed by young and old'. Lindner was convinced that *Thermobacterium mobile* was the most important fermenting agent of the tropics, and that the songs of praise to Soma really must have been 'dedicated to this *Bacterium*'. He suggested that the tropical explorers try '*TM*' in the juice of the Indian butter tree, *Bassia latifolia*, or the Ceylonese cowtree, *Gymnema lactiferum*, which have milky saps, the former sweet, the latter bitter. When Lindner himself had tried a spoonful of *TM* it had resulted in 'undiminished feeling of well-being and almost odourless excrement'.[170] Dr Leo Kaps had treated patients in the Wilheminenspital in Vienna with *TM* beer and obtained extraordinary results, and a Swedish firm and a Viennese brewery were about to produce a *TM* beer with low alcoholic content. I have found no evidence that Soma-TM-beer was in fact manufactured nor any further reference to the Lindner theory after this initial publication.

An original and, in retrospect, provocative contribution to the argument was made in 1936 by Philippe de Félice.[171] He was unable to identify Soma but he described the plant in terms that seem remarkably up-to-date: he would probably have called Soma an 'hallucinogen', had the word existed. He deduced from the record that *Sarcostemma brevistigma* and similar plants had served to replace Soma toward the end of the Vedic period, when the Indo–Iranians in emigration were forced to use new drugs in place of Soma. Alcoholic drinks such as *súrā*, he thought, might also have come to be used. Then he continues:

> Instead of indulging in suppositions that no document supports, ought we not rather to ask ourselves whether,

to arrive at the drink that plunged them into ecstasy, the ancient Indo-Iranians did not have recourse, like so many other primitive peoples, to some plant whose toxic properties they had discovered? This is what the examination of the texts seems to make clear. The liquor about which they speak is always drawn from a plant. This plant grows on the mountains which, as time passes, seem to become more and more distant, more and more inaccessible.[172] What serves to produce the mystical potion is neither the leaves nor the fruit, but always the stems. The juice is either red or clear yellow. It must be filtered or decanted, to eliminate certain elements that are disturbing or that perhaps risk rendering it too toxic. Sometimes it has a bad taste or even smacks of carrion; thus it is certainly not for pleasure that one drinks it. The inebriation that it provokes can present grave dangers: the spirit wanders, the drink can lead even to madness. It happens sometimes that the inebriation is accompanied by organic disturbances, which are in reality symptoms of an acute intoxication.

Men know and fear the baleful effects of the drug, and, though he was a god, Indra himself did not escape them, since one day the Soma came forth from every opening in his body. This emeto-cathartic effect is confirmed in an old book of Hindu medicine . . .

One may conclude from all this, it seems to us, that from the most remote antiquity the Indo–Iranians, when they were still dwelling together in their original home, possessed a special beverage reserved exclusively for the ceremonies of their religion and drawn from a toxic plant. The information that we possess about this

plant unfortunately does not permit us to determine the
species; but it is enough for us to classify it as among
the toxic plants the use of which is widespread, for
reasons of a mystical nature, in all parts of the world.

De Félice's reference to the emeto-cathartic effect of Soma
is to the epithet *vamanī* in the Āyurvedic description and
to the *Brāhmaṇa* story in which Soma injured Indra and
flowed from his mouth and 'all the openings of his vital
airs, and from his urinary tract'.[173]
Meanwhile the more conventional line of Vedic
studies continued. L. van Itallie published an article
in Dutch investigating the *Sarcostemma acidum* stalks
in the light of the Soma plant; he described acids and
alkaloids, carbohydrates and phytosterins, tannic acids
and glycosides, but drew no new conclusions.[174] Johannes
Hertel pointed out that there were many different
kinds of Soma which scientific botany was unable to
distinguish.[175] Henrik Nyberg referred to Soma–Haoma
as an intoxicating drink made from a plant no longer
identifiable, but he contributed obliquely to the *bhang*
theory with his suggestion that Zoroaster was a shaman
who drugged himself with hemp.[176] Nyberg himself,
however, distinguished clearly between Haoma and
hemp as plants, explaining Zoroaster's aversion to Haoma
in the light of the belief that Haoma-drinking induced
a state of intoxication (*Rausch*) rather than ecstasy.[177]
Joges Candra Roy then developed Mukherjee's *bhang*
hypothesis, adding to the original argument the facts
that Soma is actually called *bhang* in the ṚgVeda;[178] that
Soma is called a creeper nowhere in the ṚgVeda, but
rather an herb (*óṣadhi*), a term which could apply to

bhang; and finally that the Soma sacrifice 'was a feast and the drink added hilarity; *bhang* has been in use on similar occasions.'[179] Delli Roman Regni repeated the argument that Soma was not a fermented liquor but rather a non-alcoholic 'syrup-like thing',[180] and C. Kunham Raja maintained that, according to both the Vedas and the Avesta, Soma produced happiness (*máda*) while *súrā* produced evil intoxication (*durmáda*) and that Soma was a creeper with leaves, no longer available. Soma, he reasoned, had not time to ferment and if it had been an alcoholic drink the Indians would have substituted for it another alcoholic drink when it became unavailable, instead of the known non-alcoholic substitutes that they in fact used.[181] Yet the wine hypothesis—dead and killed again so often—reappeared in Ernst Herzfeld's *Zoroaster and his World*,[182] where he remarked that in 1931 he had received a letter from a New York gentleman who believed that a plant growing only in Persepolis—the *Salvia persepolitana*—was the Haoma, but that nothing had ever come of this communication. Herzfeld maintained that Soma must be a fermentation from grapes; that *aṃśú* means 'shoot, tendril, or bunch of grapes'; that the god Homa is the Aryan Dionysos; and that 'to thus define *homa* means to explain how wine [cultivated all over Iran before the advent of the Aryans and after] could remain unknown to the Avesta, and how the cultivation of *homa* [common in the Avesta] could disappear in Iran long before the Arab conquest. The solution is evident: *homa* is vine, wine.'[183] He adds that Haoma could not possibly be *bhang* because 'the use of hashish in Zoroaster's time is an imagination. The mysterious *homa* is wine, a reality . . . Nothing is known of the use of hemp as a narcotic prior to the Arsacid period.'[184]

Still, R.N. Chopra held to the Sarcostemma theory,[185] mentioning also the possibility of *Periploca aphylla*;[186] earlier, Chopra had also done extensive work with the Ephedras.[187] Karl Geldner in his translation of the ṚgVeda maintained that Soma could only be a species of Ephedra, probably *Ephedra intermedia* or *E. pachyclada*, the fruit of which is red and eaten by children and the stem of which is dried and taken in water as a treatment for fever.[188] Though he himself admitted that the juice was described as red, he nevertheless reiterated the old tradition that the 'milk' of the plant must be white, citing as support for this the verses that he had translated as Soma juice *mixed* with milk (IX 91[2-3] - *'nicht ganz klar'*) or Soma delighting us with the 'milk' (i.e., the expressed fluid) of the stem (IX 107[12]).

Chinnaswami Sastri published, in 1953, an article demonstrating that Soma was not wine, reviewing the *Brāhmaṇa* substitutes, and concluding that the Soma juice was neither an intoxicant nor a stimulant.[189] The orthodoxy of Sri Chinnaswami's position may be indicated by the fact that his article is written in Sanskrit. Reinhold F.G. Müller pointed out the references to Soma in the Hindu medical books and concluded that fermented drinks, *súrā*, and brandy could have been used as substitutes, but he remarked that evidence of the process of distillation in India before Islam had not been proven.[190] Mircea Eliade expresses the view that ritual intoxication by means of hemp, opium, and other plant drugs is characteristic of a decadent period of shamanism, and that such means were only reluctantly admitted into the sphere of classical

Yoga. He remarks, however, upon Patañjali's reference to herbs as a source of meditative powers and on the ṚgVedic description of the sage drinking poison.[191] He points to the use of opium and hashish in ecstatic and orgiastic sects in India, but he does not comment on Soma's possible status as such a drug, nor indeed upon the nature of the ecstasy induced by Soma, though he treats of the Vedas—and of ecstasy—at great length.[192]

A.L. Basham says that Soma is not what the Parsis now call Haoma (for the latter has no inebriating qualities), nor is it alcoholic (for it was consumed on the same day that it was pressed), and he goes on: 'The effects of Soma, with "vivid hallucinations" and the sense of expanding to enormous dimensions, are rather like those attributed to such drugs as hashish. Soma may well have been hemp . . . from which modern Indians produce a narcotic drink called *bhang*.'[193] Several Indian works were then published which investigated certain previously ignored plants as possible Soma plants: Nadkarni and Nadkarni identified the 'moon-creeper' with *Pæderia fœtida*, a plant used for the treatment of rheumatism;[194] P.V. Sharma called *Crimun latifolium*, a plant whose leaves and roots are emetic and purgative, the *som-vel*.[195]

V. G. Rahurkar arose to combat the alcohol theory, insisting that the Vedic references to *ṛjīṣá* and *tiróahnya*[196] show that Soma did not have time to ferment; he supported Oldenberg's mead hypothesis and concluded: 'Soma juice, thus, seems to be an orgiastic . . . non-alcoholic syrup-like . . . enervating drink. It was not even a fermented liquor.'[197] B.H. Kapadia says that Soma's 'fruit' is red and fleshy and liked by children;[198] that it seems to have been a creeper (he cites *atasá* and *vána*);[199] and that it is an inflexible bush with dense, upright, leafless stalks. Still, Pentii Aalto states that Soma fermented for one to nine days; 'the alcohol percentage cannot have been high. Perhaps the juice of the plant contained narcotic ingredients.'[200]

The possible nature of these 'narcotic ingredients' was the subject of an article by Karl Hummel, who gave Vedic citations to establish that the Soma plant must be mountainous, yielding copious sap and golden red in colour.[201] Noting the opinions of Regel and Sir Aurel Stein, Hummel maintained that rhubarb best satisfied the requirements, for rhubarb is known to grow in the mountains of inner Asia, to yield a copious green–gold sap that turns reddish brown after standing for a while, and, of course, to be bright red, or, in some species, golden. Moreover, rhubarb is known to contain the drug Emodin; the problem of the supposed sweetness of the Soma juice, a quality absent from rhubarb juice, is easily solved by the assumption that the Indo–Aryans mixed Soma with honey, as well as with barley and milk. And as for intoxicating properties, also absent from the rhubarb juice, Hummel maintained that these were sufficiently supplied by the mere *sight* of the glorious red stalks in the eyes of 'the naive people'. A more conventional source of intoxication—i.e., fermentation—was cited by N.A. Qazilbash to support his choice for Soma—*Ephedra pachyclada*.[202] Qazilbash maintained that the absence of latex in the Ephedra did not disqualify' it, for only the later Sanskrit writers, and never the R̥gVeda, attributed the presence of latex to the Soma plant. *Ephedra pachyclada* grows abundantly all along the Hindu Kush and Suleman ranges and yields a number of alkaloids, including L-ephedrine, Ephedra and

Pseudo-ephedrine, which act similarly to the hormone adrenalin and are used (in the form of crushed green twigs of *Ephedra pachyclada*) in Khyber and parts of Afghanistan as aphrodisiacs; it was Qazilbash's belief that at the time of the ṚgVeda the Ephedra plant was allowed to ferment, yielding a liquor that contained alcohol and ephedra alkaloids; 'the liquor, therefore, was intoxicating and possessed invigorating and stimulating effects . . . [and] . . . aphrodisiacal effects.'[203]

G.M. Patil remarks upon Soma's unparalleled intoxicating and invigorating nature. 'This intoxicant made [the Vedic people] talkative and inspired them to fight. It made them forget their mental and physical agonies, and therefore, it was a wonderful herb . . .'[204] Jan Gonda reiterated the hydromel theory,[205] and Alain Daniélou at first supported the theory of Soma as the creeper *Sarcostemma brevistigma*,[206] but later he seems to have amended his views in favour of Indian hemp (*'le chanvre Indien'*) as the plant from which the ancient Soma drink was made.[207] Yet the growing dissatisfaction with conventional theories of Soma and increasing familiarity with drug-induced religious experiences have led many modern scholars to venture onto new territory; Leopold Fischer suggests that the state of mind evinced by the Soma texts 'comes much closer to alkaloid drug experiences than to alcoholic intoxication'.[208]

It is ironic that one of the earliest Vedic beliefs about Soma—that it was brought by a bird[209]—appears as a scientific criterion in two of the most recent studies of the Soma plant. Varro E. Tyler discards *Periploca aphylla* as a possibility because it 'occurs only at low altitudes in the mountains, contains a gummy latex not utilizable as a beverage, and lacks fleshy fruits attractive to birds . . . [Soma's] fruits are eaten by birds which disperse the seeds in the mountains, thereby propagating the plant.'[210] He also discards the Ephedra theory because 'it is very difficult to express much juice from these xeromorphic plants', though he adds that *Ephedra pachyclada* when boiled in milk is used as an aphrodisiac and that 'the ash of the plant is mixed with tobacco to produce an intoxicating mixture which is applied to the gums'. Bringing similar objections against the rhubarb plant, he concludes: 'Either the ancient hymns of the *Rigveda* and the *Avesta* are gross exaggerations of fact or there grows in the vast mountain ranges of north-west India a plant whose CNS-stimulating properties, so well-known to the old inhabitants, still remain hidden from modern man.'[211]

A far more thorough article was published in the same year by J.G. Srivastava, but he too held fast to the importance of the agency of the bird, and to another long-disputed criterion: the ṚgVedic verse that some have misinterpreted as attributing to the Soma plant a thousand boughs.[212] He supports the latter implication with a verse from the *Rājanighaṇṭu* which according to him describes the climber as having 'several stems from the root-stock',[213] and with a verse from the *Suśruta Saṃhitā* which gives the Soma plant 'a tuberous root'.[214] Granting however that the ṚgVeda itself never attributes to the plant the qualities of a climber or milky latex, Srivastava goes on to mention several other plants with which the Soma has been identified, including the *Centella asiatica, Cocculus hirsutus* (used as a laxative and a cure for venereal diseases), *Fraxinus floribundus, Psoralea corylifolia* (used to cure leprosy), *Cæsalpinia*

crista, and Thespesia lampas—most of these cited by the
Āyurvedic Kosh. He disqualifies the genus Sarcostemma
and the *Periploca aphylla* because birds do not disperse
their fruits; he disqualifies Vitis vinifera because it does
not have the 'twigs and stalks' that 'the *Rig-veda* clearly
states' to have been used; and finally he settles back
upon the Ephedra, whose 'seeds are covered by red,
succulent, edible bracts, and are dispersed by birds',
and whose medical properties—which he describes at
length—are commensurate with the fame of the Soma
plant.[215]

Most recently, an article by J.P. Kooger appeared to
summarize briefly the major Soma theories, including
Wasson's *Amanita muscaria* thesis, based on the note
presented by Wasson in 1966 at the Peabody Museum of
Natural History at Yale University. Referring to Wasson's
theory as 'sensational' (*opzienbarende*) and likely to deal
a great blow to extant theories, he nevertheless concluded
that the mystery surrounding the identity of the Soma
plant was by no means solved.[216]

Some years ago, R.C. Zaehner revived the rhubarb
suggestion by referring to Haoma in these rather qualified
terms: 'The Haoma plant (from its description as yellow
and glowing probably something very like our rhubarb,
which is found in the Iranian mountains to this day) . . .'[217]
More recently, he mentioned to me the possibility that
Haoma might be the wild chicory, which grows in the
mountains of Persia, though he considers this suggestion
merely a shot in the dark. But in actual fact, what else
have all the other theories been but just that? Some
ingenious, some thoughtful, some obviously silly, some
plausible, some vague, some stubbornly wrong-headed,

some Procrustean, some groping toward the truth—but all shots in the dark.

Not knowing what plant the poets of the ṚgVeda had in mind, modern scholars have often jumped to the conclusion that the hymns are vague and obscure in speaking of Soma. The *Brāhmaṇas*, dealing as they do with involved chains of substitutes, add to the confusion in almost geometric progression; the few Avestan parallels are rendered more or less useless by the overlay of purely Iranian elements; and by the time the Europeans enter the scene, with their fixed ideas and various axes to grind, the situation approaches bedlam. Handicapped by a rudimentary knowledge of the vernacular and ancient languages of India and by inadequate communication in the academic world, scholars covered the same ground over and over again. Time and time again, the same ideas appear, are disproved, and reappear as if they were proven theories; scholars draw upon the work of their colleagues and occasionally upon newly discovered primary materials, but there is remarkably little attention to the ṚgVeda itself. (Hillebrandt, Roth and Geldner are notable exceptions.) Even within these limits, there seems to have been little contact between botanists and Vedists, Indian scholars and Europeans.

Fairly convincing evidence that Soma was not an alcoholic beverage was established quite early, yet Europeans continued to identify it with various forms of alcohol, and Indians continued to put pen to paper in order to assure the world that wine—which is of course anathema to an orthodox Hindu—was not Soma. The word for intoxication is ambiguous both in Sanskrit (*máda*) and in European languages; it denotes drunkenness or inebriation resulting from alcohol, but it may also apply to a mental state *similar* to that produced by alcohol. Thus, the statement that Soma was 'intoxicating' as it appears in various discussions and in the ṚgVeda itself does not really exclude *any* plant capable of producing a state of exhilaration, including narcotic or psychotropic plants. The further vagueness of such terms as 'liquor' and 'strong spirits' blurred the distinction between fermentation and distillation, as does the uncertain connotation of the term *súrā*. All of this served to mask the inappropriateness of the identification of Soma with alcohol.

Often scholars tended to confuse the question of the identity of the plant with the nature of the process by which the drink was made from it, overlooking the fact that the beer theory, the mead theory, and the Sarcostemma theory are complementary rather than opposed, while only such theories as those postulating wine or *bhang* exclude all others. And, on the other hand, this failure to distinguish substance from method led several scholars to attempt a combination of various theories that are in fact incompatible.

It was difficult to resist the temptation to identify the Vedic plant with the plant actually used by the descendants of the authors of the Vedas, no matter how many facts argued against this identification; and in fact one is inclined to believe that there must be *some* relationship between the original and the substitutes, some quality in the substitute which resembled a quality of Soma enough for it to have been chosen in the absence of Soma, but the question remains as to which quality—taste or colour or effect or shape—this might conceivably be.

B.H. Kapadia remarked, 'Many Latin names are given for this plant like Ephedra, etc., but we do not know exactly about it', and this could surely stand as the epitaph for the greater part of the research done in those halcyon days of science—the nineteenth century, particularly the nineteenth century in Germany—when one still felt that by giving a categorizing Latin name to an unknown quantity one had somehow settled something. To argue whether Soma was *Sarcostemma brevistigma*, *Ephedra pachyclada* or *Periploca aphylla* was to assure oneself that the Soma plant had been found and that there only remained a few messy details to be cleared up; this led to smugness and a general disinclination to delve further that might not have existed had one been forced to call the plant 'milkweed' or 'some sort of rue'. It is at first striking that *bhang* was not considered a possibility until 1921, but it is more understandable when one takes into consideration the greater attention that the psycho–physiological effects of drug-taking have received in recent times, especially in contrast with the universal disapprobation with which they were formerly associated.[218] Only in the last few generations have the anthropologists, botanists and pharmacologists of the West fully entered into the problems presented by psychotropic plants and their role in the history of human cultures. The use of hashish in the Middle East has, of course, long been known, but until twenty years ago, only as a curiosity. The discovery of mescaline by [scholars of] the modern world is almost a century old and, for some years, has provoked widespread attention.

Aldous Huxley, one of the leading writers on this subject in recent times, gave the name 'Soma' to an unspecified

marvellous drug in his novel *Brave New World*, in 1932.
In his last novel, *Island* (1962), he depicted a Utopia that
is clearly Indian throughout—Sanskrit is the language of
the cult, Śiva is worshipped, and Yoga is essential to the
philosophy of the islanders. And the drug upon which the
cult of the Island is based is a hallucinogenic mushroom.
That the mushroom is yellow and traditionally collected
high in the mountains might suggest that Huxley had
Amanita muscaria in mind—even that he was thinking of
the Soma of the ṚgVeda, although he says expressly that
the 'moksha–medicine' (as it is called) is *not* one of 'those
lovely red toadstools that gnomes used to sit on'.[219] Later
in 'Culture and the Individual'[220] Huxley, discussing the
genesis of *Island*, says that he had been thinking of 'a
substance akin to psilocybin', the active agent in the divine
mushrooms of Mexico. The Wassons played a major part
in the re-discovery of the Mexican psilocybin cult and
Wasson himself had discussed his Mexican mushrooms
and the Soma problem with Huxley in the late 1950s.

Certainly, as soon as one rids oneself of the
assumption that anything 'intoxicating' must be alcoholic,
a hallucinogen of some kind seems the likely candidate
for Soma, far more likely than millet or Afghan grapes
or rhubarb or any other of the many plants that have
been suggested. Few Vedic scholars knew any botany
and some of them may not have realized that they were
dealing with a problem primarily botanical. The botanists
on the other hand could not read the ṚgVeda, by far the
most important source about Soma, and so they permitted
themselves to enter upon speculations that often seem
ludicrous in the light of the Vedic hymns. But on behalf
of both Vedists and botanists it is only fair to recall that

for the most part the Soma question had for them merely a peripheral interest. Though the identification of Soma remained a desideratum of Indian studies, no outstanding figure applied himself directly and fully to the solution of this enigma. The historians of religion seem likewise to have given it only glancing attention.

Philippe de Felice, in 1936, offered a significant description of Soma, but, as he was not a member of the academic establishment, little notice was taken of it. Much the same is true of Huxley's speculative writings on the subject. If professional scholars attached little importance to the theories of these 'outsiders', it must be said that they offered no satisfactory alternative. Although the effort to identify the Soma plant has produced one of the most spirited and imaginative chapters in Vedic studies, it has also resulted in considerably more confusion than clarification. Wasson's novel solution to this old question revivifies a body of speculation that has become increasingly sterile and repetitive, and throws important problems of Indo–European and even Eurasian cultural history into a new perspective. This is indeed a welcome contribution, and it is to be hoped that its implications will be exploited in wide-ranging debate and fresh syntheses.

K. Ayyappa Paniker in conversation
with A.K. Ramanujan

Renowned Malayali scholar, literary critic and poet K. Ayyappa Paniker (1930–2006) recorded a conversation with A.K. Ramanujan at the University of Chicago in 1982. For years, the audiotape was kept at Paniker's residence in Trivandrum. About 20 years later, when I was a PhD researcher at the University of Kerala, Paniker entrusted me with the task of transcribing and editing this conversation for publication. Except for a few inaudible phrases, the entire interview was published in its original conversational form in 2002 in the *Journal of Literature and Aesthetics*[1] from Kollam, Kerala. The interview was highlighted by John Oliver Perry in his review article of the *Oxford India Ramanujan* in the following terms: 'An enormously revealing interview . . . There is much more of AKR's unaffectedly self-aware and self-critical "way of thinking" (and being) in this interview to ponder . . .'[2]

Here is a revised edition of the conversation between two seminal south Indian poets, thinkers and scholars of the same generation. They were both in their early fifties at the time and at a mature stage of their lives and vocations as influential poet scholars. Paniker had already become one of Kerala's most celebrated modern poets in Malayalam and a reputed academic; Ramanujan had accomplished a successful career in America as a professor of South Asian Studies, folklorist, translator and bilingual poet. Much of the discussion in this interview revolves around issues that relate to the poems and essays published in this volume, and, moreover, we believe they are still very relevant to contemporary literary criticism. There is more food for thought to dig into as we listen to Ramanujan's ideas and conceptions as a poet and translator in his 'personal voice'.

Guillermo Rodríguez

~

Ayyappa Paniker (AP): Do you still write in both languages (English and Kannada)?

A. K. Ramanujan (AKR): I write in both languages, but I have not written much in Kannada. The last thing I did was a short novel in Kannada. It is called in Kannada *Another Man's Autobiography*. In 1969 I wrote *Hokkullali Huvilla*, which literally means 'no lotus in the navel'. It is taken from a sixteenth-century Kannada work about Padmanabha. When Draupadi sees Krishna, she says in Kannada, '*Hokullali huvilla*'. I was very taken with the way the absence of the lotus was put into Kannada. You see, that is the theme, no longer mythical: the presence of a god without a lotus. It is particularly good because it was a kind of entirely mythic character being ordinary. Putting it into Kannada was the right thing to have done. My book of poems is about demythologization, so I made it *Hokkullali Huvilla*. It is also about the presence of whatever one calls 'divine' in our ordinary life [*sic*], that is, the experience that is slightly different from it. My new book of poems in English is also about that paradox. I am going to call it *Soma*.

AP: Now, I thought Chicago is the right place to talk about your career as a writer because of many reasons. I do not know much about your pre-Chicago phase. Were you writing poems in English before that?

AKR: Yes, my first poems were published in 1955 in *The Illustrated Weekly*. I did not publish much. It never occurred to me; it just happened.

AP: Did coming to Chicago or coming to the United States do it?

AKR: I do not know if that's what did it; of course, that is four years after that.

AP: Living among Indians—English as a foreign language in India—may not give you the kind of confidence that is required to write poetry.

AKR: But most of the poems that were written in this privacy were all written in India—almost all of them. My drafts and so on—most of it was done before 1960. And I reworked them a lot here.

AP: Living among native English speakers later in America might have had some influence, don't you think? You just referred to your writing in Kannada and your writing in English. You could not do both at the same time in America, I suppose, since it has something to do with the environment—the linguistic environment.

AKR: But I have written a lot of Kannada here, too, in America. It always amazes me how we contain it within ourselves—culture. It sort of even humbles me, too, to know that it's all inside here. [When] you talk to me about something in India, I know it right away. I think it has to do with the way we are interiorized. Culture is there all the time, and the language, too.

AP: I think poetry is different from the culture. Culture [is something] everybody has, but not everybody writes poetry.

AKR: That is true. Yet the culture inside one, I think, the culture as well as language, is something which you learn so early.

AP: Yet when you write in English, you don't have the same kind of cultural identification, or link-up, or belonging, as you have when you write about India. And you can write in English without having to belong to the English culture.

AKR: Because there is no language–race–culture, all three are independent. You can belong to a different race and have a [different] language, or belong to a different culture and belong to a different race. In fact, whenever you identify any of them, you get into problems. If you identify the Aryan race with a language, you get the whole Aryanization. It's the same with race and culture. I would not identify them; I would separate them somehow.

AP: Is poetry part of language or culture?

AKR: I think it's somewhere between the two. You use a language to express a culture. Culture is also like a language; culture is exactly like a second language, exactly signifiers, or the things that express elements. The expressive elements are not necessarily words in a culture; they can be clothing, they can be certain kinds of ideas, motifs, mythological things, certain conceptions of characters—these are all parts of our language, but ... not in the original linguistic sense. Because it's between the two of them that we get our entire repertoire of expression, between language and culture.

AP: Yes, you may be an expert in one language and also be an expert in another language. It is the same culture you probably express in whatever language [you speak].

AKR: Being an expert is different from being a native. To learn English well is to learn English semantics as well as English grammar, and to learn the semantics, there is no way of using it creatively without getting a lot of it inside you, right? I don't mean to speak like an Englishman.

AP: Theoretically, I quite agree with that, but let me put it this way: You write both in Kannada and in English. Is it the same culture that is expressed in English poetry and in Kannada poetry?

AKR: I think there are different emphases. It is the same person, certainly, who is writing. And, you know, culture as a purely public, social creation is not what I am talking about. It is what I call a repertory, a repertoire of images, ideas or preoccupations, prejudices even, which are shared. But ultimately, it has to come through me. Because I experience all this through the limits of whatever education I have, as well as whatever temperament, inheritance—whatever I have. So it is *that* which is really talking. Culture doesn't write poetry, I mean, you and I do, right?

AP: So, it is a personal voice. Is it the same personal voice we hear in your Kannada poetry and in your English?

AKR: I think it is different. Partly because of different traditions . . . [that] come into play. You see, one doesn't write in English simply in a vacuum. When I write it, I have learned English in the English tradition. I know English, English literature, and I have read a great deal of whatever has been written about English literature and so on. So, although I don't want to fit into it or anything like that, the English tradition is also part of my repertoire. Yet I don't want to go back to that kind of mind stock or what I write about. One is actually afraid of repeating it or imitating it too much. Somehow to carve one's own language, one's own repertoire, out of these general, public repertoires that other poets have, that all men who speak English or Kannada have, is somehow a big task and that's the difficulty. And when I am doing it in Kannada—I am also reasonably read in Kannada—when I say *Hokkullali Huvilla*, it's not a translation of Shakespeare; it's a reference to a sixteenth-century Kannada work. Or when I play with the language in Kannada, or that particular play of Sanskrit and Kannada which happens in Kannada writing. Just as I do in English wherever I can play with Latin and Anglo–Saxon, which is the English double lexical tradition. So, in those ways, the voice will be different. And along with it will come different preoccupations.

AP: But isn't Kannada the mother tongue?

AKR: Even that is a bit of a problem for me. Tamil is my mother tongue in a literal sense, and Kannada was a regional language, also my childhood language.

AP: In any case, English is not your first language. Some of the problems of second-language poetry, I believe, are certainly different from those of second-language fiction. Because poetry expresses something more intimate or more personal. Even with narrative poetry, it is bound to be a bit more personal than fiction. The personal voice of the writer may not be reflected in . . . second-language poetry, that is, in poetry written in a language other than one's mother tongue, to the same extent as it is in the mother tongue.

AKR: Fiction is also poetic. And in certain ways, fiction is very difficult to write in a second language. Partly because fiction, certainly modern fiction, is bound to reality in a very important way. You have to get tones, dialects. As a translator of fiction, I had great trouble translating Kannada fiction and Tamil fiction because you have to conflate all kinds of differences in the original language: for instance, I know a particular dialect the moment someone speaks; on a page, I know this is a Brahmin or this is a particular kind of Brahmin, and all the rest of it.

AP: Yes, and the problem of dialect you find in poetry, too. Isn't the personal voice more insistent in poetry?

AKR: Right, it is, but I don't know if 'personal' is the right word because it is a kind of persona that speaks in poetry rather than the person. It is not just Ramanujan who is speaking, but it is a fictional voice, ultimately, which only represents some parts of me, not all of me.

AP: The fictional voice in your Kannada poetry is different from the fictional voice we hear in your English poetry.

AKR: It is. It is a different selection.

AP: Is it purely linguistic?

AKR: Some of it is. Of course, linguistic—purely linguistic—I wouldn't know what to do with that because there is no such thing. Because [the] linguistic is expressive of other parts of me. What is linguistic is also expressive. For instance, it's a different kind of experimental poetry I write in Kannada.

AP: In English, you don't try to be that experimental?

AKR: I don't know; even the word 'experimental' is a problem. It's experimental in the sense that it's different from other English writers, other people writing in English, and to that extent, it has to be experimental.

AP: I mean the degree of self-confidence with which you can play with words, create words which have not existed before, combine words, etc.

AKR: I don't do that in Kannada either. I don't create new words because I don't believe in that, because I think that is another activity. I want to write the language as fully as possible, as it exists. That is very important to me when I work in English.

AP: The creative freedom, is it the same in both languages?

AKR: No two things are exactly [the] same. I am also reacting, as I was saying, to different traditions and the problems are different. In some other way, it is similar. When I am writing in English, I am also writing at the same time about my so-called Indian experience, my personal experiences for which it is often very hard to find words in English. But I still have to express it; I am constantly preoccupied with Indian folktales, Indian customs, all kinds of things. And they are, as I was saying, my repertoire—all my experiences, in the Kannada language or Tamil, and all the rest of it. Still, when I am writing in English, I won't publish anything unless I feel this has said something which is true to me. And if it has to be true to me, it has to be true to this double experience I have—my living in this country or this point of view I have *and* my Indian experience—because that experience is not something left behind; it's still here, still going on, both in my family and in the way I think and in my studies. And I am still constantly preoccupied with Indian work, whether of the present or the past, translation or whatever. So it's not something in the past for me. And when I am writing, I don't believe it is just that I am writing about India because I was an Indian child, but because India is present to me. My entire way of looking at things is constantly changed by my study of it, my feeling of it. Yesterday, I talked about the Mahabharata. All day I was preoccupied with it, and it's strange why one should be walking around in Chicago buying groceries and this and that and still be preoccupied with something in the Mahabharata. But that's the way the mind is. Just as I might have been—as I indeed was—preoccupied with Shakespeare living in Mysore. You know, to me only from some external point of view this is paradoxical and ironic; but from the internal point of view, both these traditions are equally real. But writing in Kannada has the opposite problem. The problem is, I am far away from the language. And I am writing it here, and only I am both the audience and the creator of those poems when I write them. And so the problem is that, in a way, I am much more self-conscious about the language. It's a peculiar reversal that happens.

AP: Are you self-conscious when you write in Kannada?

AKR: Yes, in Kannada, because I am aware. On the other hand, if it was entirely self-conscious, I wouldn't be able to write at all. I am actually afraid of the time when I won't be able to write because I would have to go back and feel. Unless I feel this is a language about which I do not have to think, I cannot write in it. And that is why I do not write in Kannada all the time, only at particular times when poems begin to come to me in Kannada. Then I do not think about Kannada. That's what I meant by saying that my English is switched off. I use English for my daily purposes, but my writing was all in Kannada when I wrote that novel (*Another Man's Autobiography*). Every morning, I wrote Kannada. When I began the day, before I did anything else, I wrote a few pages in Kannada, and Kannada would run in my head just as Mahabharata did yesterday. It's like that. So, I am amazed by the fact that one is able to do it, that one doesn't lose it. Partly because I read Kannada all the time, as I read Tamil and English; these three languages, which are all I have, I keep up.

AP: If you are in Mysore, there is a sense of a living audience likely to read what you write immediately after you have written or published something. That, I think— as a kind of barometer or controlling device—that kind of thing you don't have here. Whereas English is a spoken language here for you, and you hear many native speakers speak it.

AKR: But then the problem with English is that I have also had to escape that, a clichéd native speech, somehow. Because, as all poets know, if you live too long in a living language, your language becomes clichéd. Somehow, you have to renew it. It is current but not necessarily expressive.

AP: So in the case of Kannada, the problem is exactly the opposite of your problem in English. In English, you have to cut off certain things, chop off certain things to refine the dialect of the time, in a way, whereas in the other case, from the living tradition, from the literary text, you have to evolve a living language for your poetry.

AKR: But on the other hand, that living time is within me. If not, I wouldn't be able to write. If it was completely textual, I would simply enjoy reading it and let it go at that. Because my Kannada, just as I try in English, tries to be close to speech. In fact, that is the one measure I have for my Kannada writing: 'Can I say it? Can I say it ordinarily?' That is what is experimental about my Kannada writing. Even the experimental writers in Kannada, I think, do not go as far with their use of language as I do. Because that's the only test I have for its being alive. I say it to myself. I say, 'Can I say this to someone?' But if you apply that too rigorously, you get a rather different kind of poetry.

AP: Your English poems cannot be thought of as some kind of translation of your Kannada poems, I suppose?

AKR: I cannot translate them at all. I have tried translating one into the other and I can't do it.

AP: Take a poem like 'Inchworm', which we have translated and published in Malayalam. It was originally written in Kannada, but the title 'Inchworm' makes one think that it was quite possible for you to have written it in English as well. If I remember right, there is nothing, apparently, that prevents you from writing that poem in English as well, but the fact is you did write it in Kannada.

AKR: Yes, I read that story first in a children's book here, and of course that pointed to other uses of the story about literature, about criticism and all that. It's about all that, the whole business of measuring. [The inchworm] measures with the whole length of its body, and its body becomes the measure and so on. All of that—all those notions—started stirring me, and the poem came to me in Kannada.

AP: In the same way some of your poems in English could as well have been written in Kannada, I mean from a reader's point of view, not from your point of view. What are some of the conditions which might have—not these accidents, I suppose—prevented you from writing one thing in Kannada and the other in English?

AKR: I have worried about that. But, of course, the whole problem is [that] you do not choose your language. I don't think poems can choose their language. You choose it after it has come to you, anyway. That is, you may use certain kinds of metrical elements or forms. But even those, ultimately, even those corrections have [to] somehow . . . come to you.

AP: This question of bilingualism is of great interest to Indian writers. There is Nissim Ezekiel saying he can't write in any other language, so he writes in English. Whereas in your case, that cannot be said. You write equally well in at least two.

AKR: You know, 'equally' is not the term that I would use. I write; I write in two languages. And I have doubts about that. Because sometimes I wish I had only one language. I feel that all of oneself could have been in that language. As most English writers do, to them, clearly, another language is impossible to write in. Given our cultural antecedents, we are in certain ways—I am speaking of it externally, from the point of view of our cultural history, and not internally—split between the mother tongue and the second language. And that is not new to us. In this new book of mine, *Hymns for the Drowning*, my translations have something to do with me and my preoccupations. I have a long section on relating Sanskrit to Tamil. It is exactly parallel to English and our mother tongue. It's parallel in the way the two kinds of languages work. And in the kinds of problems we have, the whole overthrow of Sanskrit in the Bhakti movement; if not overthrow, certainly the use of Sanskrit as another kind of language, and what kinds of usages we have. It's similar in other ways too. Sanskrit has enormous prestige, and the whole claim that it is pan-Indian is the same kind of claim that's made for English. Of course, to me, none of that is important. But it's a dilemma that the Indian has to face.

AP: Now, is bilingualism necessarily a handicap?

AKR: It is a resource as well as a source of anxiety. I don't know if it is a drawback, because anxiety itself is not a drawback. Even that may be a resource, you never know (laughs). But it may be simply romanticism on my part to say that.

AP: I mean questions of metre, apart from vocabulary or ideas. There are problems of prosody, problems of the music of language. Are these things in general ably handled by Indian writers in English, whether they are bilingual or monolingual?

AKR: Very few can handle it well. Very few Indian writers writing in English, for instance, can write formal verse.

AP: But should they write formal verse?

AKR: No, but it should be an option. You should not be stuck in informality, just as you should not be stuck in formality. I think an exception is Nissim Ezekiel, who can write in verse. He has always used formal verse; it's only now that he has moved to different ideas. And I have written formal verse. I have written, as experiments, various kinds of sonnets and so on. I always use rhymes, for instance. But the rhymes are usually very undefined, as I want them to be.

AP: Of course, even native, first-language English poets do that these days.

AKR: I also get that from my own Kannada and other traditions, where you do get rhymes, but the rhymes are not in rhymes. I like that; I like to hear the rhyme but not see it very often.

AP: Are there metrical restrictions which apply to Indian writers in English which may not apply to native writers in English?

AKR: Of course, their sense of rhythm is different.

AP: Is there an Indian rhythm in Indian poetry in English?

AKR: I have not studied it enough to tell you. But I'm sure there is, because our way of speaking and our sense of stress are different. For instance, very few, even very good speakers of English among us, master stress, as you know. And the English metre is a stressed metre. Very often, I myself use an accented metre in English because that's easier for me. You know, a kind of *mātrā*.[3] If you look at the regularities of my verse, I usually use very regular verse. But an English speaker may not think it is regular because he may not count syllables. I think you should ultimately use yourself as a resource, and these peculiarities are also a resource. I don't mean all the errors and so forth, because very often people use Indian English only in the sense that it is funny and full of errors. I don't believe in that. I think good speakers of English have their own rhythm. Indian English has its own rhythm, and necessarily so because the pressure of the first language is never absent in Indian English.

AP: Do you think that this was the rhythm that one could hear in Toru Dutt and Sarojini Naidu, and even Aurobindo?

AKR: No, probably not.

AP: In the post-Independence?

AKR: It's really an independence from the pure English rhythm that all of us may want to try. I don't think we need to try that. We have to be somewhere in between.

AP: So could we say that the pre-Independence writers, famous as they were in many fields, still thought of English as a foreign language?

AKR: The only thing I could say is that I am only making a guess. Because if I go back, I may find that Aurobindo has a lot of Sanskrit rhythms since he was learned in Sanskrit as well as in English.

AP: It's certainly a topic that someone has to study. Not only the rhythm of Indian English as a language but also the manipulation of these rhythms in pre-Independence poetry and post-Independence poetry.

AKR: See, I have been re-reading R.K. Narayan, for instance. Narayan, in some ways, writes very acceptable English from the English point of view in his prose. If you read him now, you will hear that, in fact, one of the resources of Narayan is the closeness of the narrative to his own speech. I don't mean as a person, but as a whole kind of person.

AP: Yes, I have often felt that in his kind of humour, peculiarly Tamil . . . humour, which is also language-based, he writes Tamil in English. That's why it succeeds. You cannot forget that he is an Indian writer with a Tamil background and so on.

AKR: And it's not accidental that the older, senior writers of Indian fiction, all three of them—Mulk Raj Anand, Narayan, Raja Rao—write English differently from an Englishman and from one another because of their backgrounds. And

I think that's where their creativity is. And they are not specifically experimental, but they are being attentive to their own beings. You can hear Kannada in *Kanthapura*, even in *The Serpent and the Rope*. Though Raja Rao himself says he would like to write in English as if it were Sanskrit. I think that is an overload. But it's really kind of in-between, between Kannada, Sanskrit and English. And there is a new rhythm that comes through. And someone like Desani, with that particular creole of Indian English, of Indians speaking English somewhat imperfectly but still creatively, with its own humour, with its own translations. The whole humour comes . . . from the interplay between Indians and English. And all three of them are like that. Narayan seems perfectly natural; you read him, you hear Tamil and all kinds of things. And that is very important to me, I think, and for Indian creativity and writing in English.

AP: Let's talk about your own translations from Tamil or Kannada into English. I do not know if you translate English into Kannada.

AKR: Yes, I translate English into Kannada also. All my writing, of course, is concerned with the three languages I have. These three I carry with me wherever I go, and they are constantly interacting. And everything I do has to respond to some part of this interaction. Whether it is to write in English, or translate or write in Kannada. In my Kannada, there is a lot of English. My English and my Tamil are not absent in my Kannada.

AP: Do you try to accommodate the rhythm of the original in your translations?

AKR: A great deal. I try. In my new book, *Hymns for the Drowning*, I . . . even [try] to accommodate the syntax of the original without breaking the English syntax. Because the language has many possibilities in syntax, though only some are favourites. For instance, English, by and large, is not left branching as Tamil is or Kannada is. And whereas modern English verse does not use parallelism so much, all the Indian poetry is built on various kinds of parallelisms, and I try to keep that. *Speaking of Siva*, for instance, is like that. Whereas, . . . classical Tamil poetry doesn't do that; it does something else. It writes, for instance, an entire poem in a single sentence, [with] everything left branching. So I have to accommodate that into English.

AP: The reader has to be aware of the fact that he is reading a translation or that he is reading a poem by an Indian poet. When you have the title *Speaking of Siva* or when you find something like Murugan in the title, then it is a signal. But there may be poems where neither the title nor the subject matter as such may obviously indicate that this is from an Indian source. What will happen to the native English reader when it comes to a point like that? Is it an encounter, a universal experience?

AKR: Even these poems, I think, are universal experiences. Otherwise, they would not be good to read.

AP: But here, of course, they have the cultural sources which give it away. So, the reader brings that consciousness with him. Is it necessary for the reader to know the background of the writer?

AKR: To some . . . extent, in order that the mental set is proper so that he doesn't misunderstand. Basically, the information that you need to read a poem is to keep you from misunderstanding or bringing your own contents to it. To me, all those prep[aration]s are really not meant to make you understand a poem but to liberate you and the poem from your own limits.

AP: To cut off irrelevant associations?

AKR: Yes, which you will bring to it naturally. But this is one reason why I try to translate groups of poems of seventy, eighty, so that the biases of single poems are in some ways lighted up or interpreted by other poems. So, I choose my poems. This is one of the reasons I have not simply done translations of all the poems, partly because not all of them come through for me. I do not experience all of them equally, and some of them I don't know how to translate. I translate double or triple the number and publish the ones . . . [that] I think will work as English poems and . . . are also somehow faithful to the original. And I also choose them from the point of presenting the world of the original poems. Look at something like *The Interior Landscape*. There will be poems from all . . . five landscapes, and what the classical rhetoricians mention regarding the different themes, you will . . . also [find] a variety of themes in there. So I chose them very carefully. It's the same with *Speaking of Siva*. I didn't do one poet, or just a few poems. Each poet has a kind of graph in his mystical ascent which is different from the others'. All of them speak about Siva, but different aspects of Siva. One is very much about the beauty of Siva and so on.

That's why this new book of mine is about a Vaishnavite
poet. There are about a thousand poems in Nammāḻvār's
Tiruvāymoḻi, and I have chosen about ninety poems for
Hymns for the Drowning.

AP: Why do you have this title about 'drowning'?

AKR: Because the word 'al' in 'Āḻvār' means 'to drown',
as well as 'to sink', as well as 'to immerse'. So, it's not his
body that drowns, though I make a distinction between
being immersed and being drowned. And also, there is the
notion that the immersed ones are talking to the ones who
are drowning. They know how to manage it in some way;
they have to survive, come alive through the immersion,
whereas the rest of us simply drown. That's why I call
it *Hymns for the Drowning*. Actually, this is where the
English comes in. I had that great passage by Conrad in
mind where he distinguishes immersion from drowning.

AP: There is a conscious possession of the situation,
which you have put before you are taken possession of by
the situation.

AKR: Right, one is also surrendering to the element, in
a way, and not fighting it, and so one is also part of it.
The poems are full of these situations. There is also one
particular poem where the Āḻvār is literally drowning
and the Lord comes and saves him. So there are different
possibilities for that. People might think that I have
stretched the word a bit, but I think it's a nice title. So
it's not the Āḻvārs who are drowning, though there is a
poem about the Āḻvārs drowning, but I think it's also the

reader. Because they talk a great deal about that, about saving the reader

AP: The water image is also there—the waters of faith?

AKR: Water is a central element in Vishnu mythology, and it's very much there. And the name Narayana, the Lord of the Waters. He sleeps on the water.

AP: There is one more thing I would like to discuss with you. You being a linguist, a professionally trained linguist, and being a teacher, can be something between a hindrance and a help in the writing of poetry. And the self-consciousness, living perhaps in an urban environment in Chicago. We started by talking about Chicago and we['ve] come back to Chicago. What is the 'interior landscape' here, living in Chicago as a professor of languages?

AKR: You see, linguistics is not a hindrance in the sense that to be a hindrance is to be self-conscious about the particulars of the language you are writing in. A lot of the linguistics I do is very theoretical and applies to the study of poetry [and] things like that. I really believed in the way great poems are structured, the way language works in poetry, in a passage of Shakespeare, etc. Of course, there will be poems that fail . . . [due to] too much self-consciousness, and they do fail sometimes. And when they do, I hope I'll have the good sense not to publish them.

AP: Well, academic life can turn poems into academic exercises.

AKR: No, not true. Actually, reading too much criticism can. Then you begin to write for the critic.

AP: You don't think of your poetry as academic exercises at all—not even your translations, of course.

AKR: I don't think so. I would do a very different kind of translation. I would not take that long. It takes me five to ten years to do a small book of translations and I translate only what I absolutely love—some things . . . [that] possess me, that are different from other poems. But you need a certain amount of scholarship to understand them. For instance, I don't translate something I already know. I'm . . . in discovery of new poems all the time, from first century Tamil, eighth century Tamil, twelfth century Kannada and so on. So, I need some scholarship for that, but fortunately, I have studied these languages for so long that it no longer seems like scholarship to me. I can read all of them comfortably.

AP: Sanskrit poems written by other people in the past had some academic elements in them. Does that apply to Indian writing in English? Are they mostly academic, literary?

AKR: Some, I think. Of course, that's bound to happen in any writing. In Kannada or Tamil, there is academic writing. That's always a danger. The whole business about learning a language is to reach a point where it doesn't sound as if it is learned. I don't know if one has reached that, but that's the dream, isn't it? To write one's native language as if one is not fully native and to write a foreign language as if one is not a foreigner. That's what I'm saying about Kannada and English. One has to renew the native language to a kind of refinement or expressiveness which somebody who is nearly native in the language cannot attain. And singularly because we need to immerse ourselves enough in [a] foreign, so-called foreign language, or by whatever accidents like mine we are immersed in, so that we no longer think about it. When I'm talking to you, I am not aware I'm speaking in English.

AP: So you can also get drowned in language or be immersed in it and afraid of drowning; using a language is parallel to what the Vaishnavite poets speak about, when they refer to 'any experience'.

AKR: I think so. And to do that without self-consciousness, without academic doctrine is difficult. It is a particular danger for us; it's hard for us.

AP: Who are some of the Indian poets in English who are less academic?

AKR: Only the ones who have been well recognized now, like Nissim or Parthasarathy and Daruwalla, I would say, are not academic at all.

AP: Of course, the danger is always there of dipping into the academic.

AKR: Because all of them, at one time or another, have been English teachers, except probably Jayanta Mahapatra.

Even Daruwalla, I think, has a degree in English and probably comes from a background of English literature.

AP: Do you think Indian poets in English are now being influenced by English or American poets at all? I mean, at least the poets of your generation.

AKR: I read them from the library, but of course, not many of them are good writers. I think to a large extent they are influenced in their use of free verse or three-line stanzas and so on, which have all precedents in American or English poetry. And there is nothing wrong with that.

AP: Young Indian writers of poetry in English, I find, are [more] influenced . . . by Indian writers like you. Writers of your generation are influencing younger writers. I think they read more of your work than English or American poets.

AKR: I didn't know that. In some ways, that is quite natural, because I'm sure they hear the voice more clearly. Also, the experiences that we talk about may be closer to . . . [theirs]. And that's the kind of experience they want to fashion into poems.

AP: Are you particularly fond of any living English or American writers?

AKR: I read a lot of them. At different times, I read different ones. I have read a lot of Williams, Stevens and among the older ones, Yeats.

AP: And the younger ones after Williams and Stevens? Living writers, contemporary ones?

AKR: What have I been reading . . . last week I've been reading Galway Kinnell. And Robert Bly.

AP: Bly has his own methods of translation, which I think are very different from your methods, am I right?

AKR: That's right. I think, partly because his translations from languages he knows are different from the languages he doesn't know. I think when he translated something like Kabir, for instance, he translated a translation of a translation. He took Tagore's translation, which itself was not directly written by him; somebody else had done it for him. But then, that's only one side of translation. Of course, there should be a translation that reads well, better than one that doesn't read well. Even if it's not quite faithful sometimes. But I wish he were faithful; I wish he would work with a Hindi speaker; and I think he could do something marvellous.

AP: Is translation more difficult than original poetry?

AKR: I wouldn't say that. But I'm saying it has different demands. On the one hand, it has to be a poem; on the other hand, it has to be a poem which is like the original poem . . . you don't have [that problem] if you are writing your own poem, unless you have models of some sort.

AP: Yes, one could argue that every written poem is a kind of translation of the inner experience of the poet, but this does not get written.

AKR: Or, even if you don't write poems in a vacuum, there are still models of some kind.

AP: Do you believe in the existence of poems which exist in some vague form before they are written down, you know, the 'original poem' before you express it?

AKR: I don't think so. They get created in an act of not merely writing; writing, rewriting, correcting, all of that is the process through which the poem comes into being. And before it has come into being, I don't think it exists. It exists somewhat as a disturbance, as a stir somewhere. It doesn't come through so quickly; only the first draft.

AP: So, you are a confirmed revisionist. You believe in the act of revising. Sometimes in the act of revision, one reaches that level of intensity where there might be greater spontaneity, as in Yeats.

AKR: The point I was making was that the revision has to be as involved, in the [same] fashion, as the original writing. I can't draw a line. The revision is not made out of reason and calculation; . . . everything else is spontaneous. All of it has to be a combination of both.

AP: Does the acceptance of a revised version lead to the rejection of an earlier version, or should they quite fit? Can we save them as different poems?

AKR: I think the writer saves the latest one. Others may think, 'why did he revise it like this?' But I think it's not why would he revise it. But there may be faults of taste in the revision.

AP: Tagore's translation of the *Gitanjali* is certainly far inferior to the original. And if somebody else may quote a better translation, a closer translation, both can exist and coexist. Perhaps it should be left to the reader, ultimately.

AKR: Of course, there are sometimes two versions of a poem, like some of Yeats' poems. He has two versions of a poem: an early poem, which he also redid later. They are very different; the progression is very different, and the diction is different, too.

AP: And both can survive?

AKR: Both can survive. I think they are related poems, poems of the same family.

AP: It's good to think of families of poems like that because it proves that, like the poems you translate, they hang together, they stay together. And one enriches the meaning of the other.

AKR: But I'm not sure one should publish all of one's drafts. It's a form of arrogance (laughs).

AP: It makes it easy for poets to make a living out of that.

AKR: They can, yes. And living poets do these days; they sell all their drafts . . .

Biographical Note

A.K. Ramanujan (1929–1993), born in Mysore, India, received his BA with Honors in English Language and Literature from Mysore University in 1949 and his MA the following year. For the next eight years, he was a lecturer in English successively at S.N. College, Quilon (Kerala), Thiagarajar College, Madurai (Tamil Nadu), Lingaraj College, Belgaum (Karnataka) and M.S. University, Baroda (Gujarat). In 1958, he received a graduate diploma in linguistics from Deccan College, Poona.

The following year, Ramanujan came to the United States on a Fulbright fellowship, enrolling at Indiana University, which awarded him a PhD in linguistics in 1963. He joined the faculty of the University of Chicago in 1962 as an assistant professor and was appointed professor in 1968. At the time of his death, he was the William H. Colvin Professor in the Department of South Asian Languages and Civilizations, the Department of Linguistics, and the Committee on Social Thought. He also taught as a visiting professor at Harvard University, the University of California at Berkeley, the University of Wisconsin, Madison and the University of Michigan.

Ramanujan received many honours and prizes, including the Padma Shri awarded by the Government of India in 1976 for his contributions to Indian literature and linguistics and a MacArthur Prize Fellowship in 1983. In 1988, he delivered the Radhakrishnan Memorial Lectures at All Soul's College, Oxford. He was elected to the American Academy of Arts and Sciences in 1990. In 1999, he was posthumously given the Sahitya Akademi Award in English for *The Collected Poems*.

He was the author or translator of twenty-three books, including eight posthumous works, and he co-authored and edited various other seminal publications. While still alive, he published seven volumes of original poetry in English and Kannada and landmark translations of verse from Tamil (ancient *Sangam* classics and medieval *Āḻvār* saints) and Kannada, including his famous book of poetry from medieval Kannada mystics, *Speaking of Siva* (Penguin, 1973), which was nominated for the National Book Award in the USA. His translation of U.R. Ananthamurthy's Kannada novel *Samskara* is considered a classic. His last published book during his lifetime was *Folktales from India: A Selection of Oral Tales from Twenty-Two Languages* (Pantheon, 1991).

Ultimately, the greatest honour for any writer lies in one's work being read well after life has passed. Ramanujan's poems, prose, essays and translations have left a vast legacy, as his writings continue to inspire and influence a new generation of poets and scholars, and enthrall readers to this day.

A.K. Ramanujan: Select Bibliography

1. Poetry in English
1.1. Collections

The Striders. London: Oxford University Press, 1966.
Relations: Poems. London, N. York: O.U.P., 1971.
Selected Poems. N. Delhi, N. York: O.U.P., 1976.
Second Sight. N. Delhi, N. York: O.U.P., 1986.

1.2. Posthumous collections

The Black Hen in *The Collected Poems of A.K Ramanujan*.
Ed. Vinay Dharwadker. N. Delhi: O.U.P., 1995.
Contains also *The Striders* (1966), *Relations* (1971)
and *Second Sight* (1986).
Uncollected Poems and Prose. A. K. Ramanujan. Eds.
Molly A. Daniels–Ramanujan and Keith Harrison.
London and N. Delhi: O.U.P., 2001.
The Oxford India Ramanujan. Ed. Molly Daniels–
Ramanujan. N. Delhi, O.U.P., 2004. An omnibus
collection that includes all the poems from the

previously published books of poetry in English (1966, 1971, 1986, 1995, 2001) listed above, and the four collections of poetry translations from medieval Kannada and classical and medieval Tamil (1967, 1973, 1981, 1985) listed below.

2. Posthumous collections of prose in English

The Collected Essays of A.K. Ramanujan. Gen. ed. Vinay Dharwadker. N. Delhi: O.U.P., 1999.

Uncollected Poems and Prose. Eds. Molly A. Daniels–Ramanujan and Keith Harrison. London and New Delhi: O.U.P., 2001.

Journeys: A Poet's Diary. Eds. Krishna Ramanujan and Guillermo Rodríguez. Gurgaon: Penguin Random House, 2019.

3. Books of translations
3.1. Tamil and Kannada poetry into English

The Interior Landscape: Love Poems from a Classical Tamil Anthology. Bloomington: Indiana University Press, 1967.

Speaking of Siva. N. Delhi: Penguin India, 1973,

Hymns for the Drowning: Poems for Visnu by Nammāḻvār. Princeton: Princeton University Press, 1981.

Poems of Love and War: From the Eight Anthologies and the Ten Long Poems of Classical Tamil. New York: Columbia University Press, 1985.

The Oxford India Ramanujan. N. Delhi: O.U.P., 2004.

3.2. Kannada fiction into English

Samskara: A Rite for a Dead Man (*Samskara*). By U.R. Ananthamurthy. N. Delhi: O.U.P., 1976.

3.3. English fiction into Kannada

Haladi Meenu (The Yellow Fish). By Molly Daniels. Dharwar: Manohar Granthamala, 1966.

3.4. Collections of Indian folktales in English

Folktales from India. A Selection of Oral Tales from Twenty-Two Languages. N. York: Pantheon, 1991.
A Flowering Tree and Other Oral Tales from India. Eds. Stuart Blackburn and Alan Dundes. Berkeley: U. of California Press, 1997. N. Delhi: Viking Penguin India, 1997.

4. Other co-authored or co-edited works in English

A.K. Ramanujan and Edward C. Dimock Jr. et al., eds. *The Literatures of India. An Introduction.* Chicago: Chicago University Press, 1974. London: O.U.P., 1975.
A.K. Ramanujan and Stuart Blackburn, eds. *Another Harmony: New Essays on the Folklore of India.* Berkeley: University of California Press, 1986. London: O.U.P., 1986.
A.K. Ramanujan, V. Narayana Rao and David Shulman, eds. *When God is a Customer: Telugu Courtesan Songs*

by Ksetrayya and Others. Berkeley: U. of California Press, 1994. N. Delhi: O.U.P., 1995.

A.K. Ramanujan and Vinay Dharwadker, eds. *The Oxford Anthology of Modern Indian Poetry*. N. Delhi: O.U.P, 1994.

5. Works in Kannada
5.1. Poetry collections in Kannada

Hokkulalli Hoovilla (No Lotus in the Navel). Dharwar: Manohar Granthamala, 1969.
Mattu Itara Padyagalu (And Other Poems). Dharwar: Manohar Granthamala, 1977.
Kuntobille (Hopscotch). Dharwar: Manohar Granthamala, 1990.

5.2. Novella in Kannada

Matthobhana Atmacharitre (Someone Else's Autobiography). Dharwar: Manohar Granthamala, 1978.

5.3. Collections of proverbs in Kannada

Gadegalu (Proverbs). Dharwar: Karnataka University, 1955. Dharwar: Karnataka Visvavidyalaya, 1967. Dharwar: Manohar Granthamala, 1978.

5.4. Posthumous collected works in Kannada

A.K. Ramanujan Samagra (Complete Kannada Works), eds. Ramakant Joshi and S. Divakar. Dharwar: Manohar Granthamala, 2011.

6. Translations of A.K. Ramanujan's Kannada books into English

6.1. Kannada poetry

No Lotus in the Navel (*Hokkulalli Hoovilla*, 1969). Trans. Tonse N.K. Raju and Shouri Daniels–Ramanujan. *A.K. Ramanujan. Poems and a Novella.* Advisory ed. Prithvi Datta Chandra Shobhi. N. Delhi, O.U.P., 2006, pp. 3–58.

And Other Poems (*Mattu Itara Padyagalu*, 1977). Trans. Tonse N.K. Raju and Shouri Daniels–Ramanujan. *A.K. Ramanujan. Poems and a Novella.* N. Delhi, O.U.P., 2006, pp. 59–126.

Hopscotch (*Kuntobille*, 1990).Trans. Tonse N.K. Raju and Shouri Daniels–Ramanujan. *A.K. Ramanujan. Poems and a Novella.* N. Delhi, O.U.P., 2006, pp. 127–86.

6.2. Kannada novella

Someone Else's Autobiography (*Matthobhana Atmacharitre*). Trans. Tonse N.K. Raju and Shouri Daniels– Ramanujan. *A.K. Ramanujan. Poems and a Novella.* N. Delhi, O.U.P., 2006, pp. 214–323.

Index of Titles

Index of First Lines

Notes

Foreword

1   It is possible that instead of Mahapatra, Konarak could be referring to Shiv K. Kumar, whose poem 'The Sun Temple, Konark', which appeared in *Subterfuges* (1976), Ramanujan would have known. The 'chariots of war pirouette among arrows' could be a reference to P. Lal, who translated the *Mahabharata* and whose Writers Workshop published two of Ramanujan's early books; and the 'medicine men' to Gieve Patel, who was a general practitioner, though in Bombay.

2   Molly Daniels-Ramanujan, 'An A.K. Ramanujan Story', in *The Oxford India Ramanujan* (New Delhi: Oxford University Press, 2004), pp. i–xxxvi.

Hummel's Miracle: The Search for Soma

1   A.K. Ramanujan, *Journeys: A Poet's Diary*, eds. Krishna Ramanujan and Guillermo Rodríguez (Gurgaon, Haryana, India: Penguin Random House, 2019). See 'Mescalin Notes', p. 143.

2   In 1968, the English rock band The Beatles travelled to Rishikesh and trained in Transcendental Meditation with

Maharishi Mahesh Yogi, which helped popularize Indian spirituality in the West. The band's influence at the time was so broad that even AKR mentions listening to the Beatles' *White Album* during his mescaline episode; Ramanujan, *Journeys*, p. 156.

3   R. Gordon Wasson, *Soma: Divine Mushroom of Immortality* (New York: Harcourt Brace Jovanovich, 1968).

4   A.K. Ramanujan, *The Collected Essays of A.K. Ramanujan*, ed. Vinay Dharwadker and Stuart H. Blackburn (New Delhi: Oxford University Press, 1999); see 'Men, Women and Saints', p. 279.

5   'On discovering that Soma is a mushroom'.

6   Wasson claims there are 120 Soma hymns; Wasson, *Soma: Divine Mushroom of Immortality,* p. 5.

7   Mandala or 'book' 9, out of 10.

8   Richard J. Miller, *Drugged: the Science and Culture behind Psychotropic Drugs* (New York, NY: Oxford University Press, 2014), 8. Miller, a pharmacologist, writes that Amanita muscaria means 'fly poison' and was used as an insecticide, but further inquiry showed the mushroom only temporarily stunned insects, from which they recovered.

9   Wendy Doniger O'Flaherty, 'The Post-Vedic History of the Soma Plant', in Wasson, *Soma*, 1968.

10 Frits Staal, 'How a Psychoactive Substance Becomes a Ritual: The Case of Soma', *Social Research* vol. 68, no. 3 (2001): p. 759.

11 Arthur Anthony Macdonell, *Hymns from the Rigveda* (Calcutta: Association Press, 1922), p. 78. http://www.archive.org/details/cu31924023014750.

12 Ramanujan, 'Men, Women and Saints', *Collected Essays*, p. 279.

13 *Sathapatha Brahmana*, Chowkhamba edition, 5.1.2.10; Doniger, in Wasson, *Soma,* p. 95.

14 Harry Falk, 'Soma I and II', *Bulletin of the School of Oriental and African Studies*, University of London 52, no. 1 (1989): pp. 77–90.

15 Ramanujan, *Journeys*, p. 137. He also mentions Algernon Swinburne's peyote trances, p. 156.

16 Wendy Doniger, *The Rig Veda: an Anthology: One Hundred and Eight Hymns, Selected, Translated and Annotated*, Harmondsworth, Middlesex, England: Penguin Books (1981), 8.48.1, p. 134.

17 Ibid, 8.48.3, p. 134.

18 Doniger, in Wasson, *Soma*, pp. 97–98.

19 Personal interview with Doniger, 2022.

20 Thomas J. Riedlinger, 'Wasson's Alternative Candidates for Soma', *Journal of Psychoactive Drugs* 25, no. 2 (1993): pp. 149–56. doi:10.1080/02791072.1993.10472245.

21 Doniger, *The Rig Veda*, p. 240.

22 Ibid., p. 133.

23 Wasson, *Soma*, pp. 23–24.

24 Ibid., pp. 33–34. See the preface to essay by Doniger in this volume.

25 Doniger, *The Rig Veda*, pp. 122–23.

26 Wasson, *Soma*, p. 160.

27 Terence K. McKenna, *Food of the Gods: the Search for the Original Tree of Knowledge: a Radical History of Plants, Drugs, and Human Evolution*, (New York, N.Y.: Bantam Books, 1992.), p. 111

28 McKenna, *Food of the Gods*; Riedlinger, 1993.

29 McKenna, *Food of the Gods,* p. 110.

30 Ibid., pp. 110–13.

31 David Strophlet Flattery and Martin Schwarz, 'Soma and its Legacy in Religion, Language and Middle Eastern Folklore, Near Eastern Studies', *Haoma and Harmaline. The Botanical Identity of the Indo–Iranian Hallucinogen,* vol. 21 (Berkeley/Los Angeles/London: University of California Press, 1989).

32 Matthew Clark, *Botanical Ecstasies: Psychoactive Plant Formulas in India and Beyond* (London, Psychadelic Press, 2021), p. 12.

33 Doniger, in Wasson, *Soma*, 1968.

34 Clark, *Botanical Ecstasies*, p. 12.

35 Falk, 1989.

36 Jan E.M. Houben, 'The Soma-Haoma problem: Introductory overview and observations on the discussion', *Electronic Journal of Vedic Studies* (2003). ffhalshs-02173553f

37 Staal, 2001.

38 Jayita Biswas and Rita Singh, 'Ephedra stipitate (Ephedraceae), a new species from Ladakh, India', *Annales Botanici Fennici* 59, no. 1 (2022): pp. 123–29. https://doi.org/10.5735/085.059.0119.

39 Clark Matthew James, *The Tawny One: Soma Haoma and Ayahuasca* (London, New York: Muswell Hill Press, 2017), p. 117.

40 Houben, 2003.

41 Clark, *The Tawny One*, p. 118.

42 David Spess, *Soma: The Divine Hallucinogen* (Rochester, VT: Park Street Press, 2000); Andrew McDonald, 'A Botanical Perspective on the Identity of Soma (*Nelumbo Nucifera Gaertn.*) Based on Scriptural and Iconographic Records', *Economic Botany* 58 (December, 2004): pp. 147–73.

43 McDonald, 2004.

44 Keshav Raj Paudel and Nisha Panth, 'Phytochemical Profile and Biological Activity of *Nelumbo nucifera*', *Evidence-Based Complementary and Alternative Medicine*, vol. 2015, Article ID 789124, 16 pages (2015). https://doi.org/10.1155/2015/789124.

45 Clark, *The Tawny One*, p. 157.

46 Clark, *Botanical Ecstasies*, p. 19.

47 Ibid., p. 34.

48 Sariandi published books and articles on his research in Afghanistan, Bactria and Margiana for decades, until he died in 2013. Bactria and Margiana were Greek names used for territories in what is now Turkmenistan.

49 M.D. Merlin, 'Archaeological Evidence for the Tradition of Psychoactive Plant Use in the Old World', *Economic Botany*

57, no. 3 (2003): pp. 295–323. http://www.jstor.org/stable/4256701.

50　Victor I. Sariandi, 'Margiana and Soma–Hoama', *Electronic Journal of Vedic Studies*, vol. 9 Issue 1c (2003).

51　Merlin, 2003.

52　Sariandi, 2003.

53　Wendy Doniger, *The Hindus: An Alternative History* (New York: Penguin Press, 2009).

54　Flattery and Schwarz, 1989.

55　Sariandi, 2003.

56　Houben, 2003.

57　Karl Hummel, 'Review of Wasson 1969', *Studien zur Indologie und Iranistik* (1997): pp. 79–90.

58　Merlin, 2003; Houben, 2003.

59　Wasson, *Soma*, p. 16.

60　Doniger, *Hindus*, p. 122.

61　Houben included this quote as an epigraph in his essay, 'The Soma–Haoma problem', 2003.

62　Miller, *Food of Gods*, p. 6.

63　Doniger, *The Hindus*.

64　Ibid., 160–61; personal interview with Doniger, 2022.

65　'Soma (121)'

66　'On Discovering that Soma is a mushroom.'

67　'Soma.'

68　Our apartment in Chicago was half a block from 57th Street, just down the way from a small local grocery.

69　'On discovering that Soma is a mushroom.'

70　'Soma: he is converted.'

The 'Ordinary Mystery' Trip: Soma in A.K. Ramanujan's Poetry

1　See for instance Wendy Doniger, *The Rig Veda: an Anthology: One Hundred and Eight Hymns, Selected, Translated and*

Annotated, Harmondsworth, Middlesex, England: Penguin Books (1981), p. 121. See also A.K. Ramanujan's first poem in this collection, titled 'Soma (121)'.

2   See Krishna Ramanujan's introductory essay and Wendy Doniger's 1968 pioneering study 'The Post-Vedic History of the Soma Plant' reprinted in this volume.

3   R. Gordon Wasson, *Soma: Divine Mushroom of Immortality* (New York: Harcourt, Brace Jovanovich, 1968), where Wendy Doniger's essay was first published.

4   See, for instance, Allen Ginsberg's comments in a 1993 interview: 'I was very interested in soma. I had met Robert Gordon who had a lot of experience of mushrooms and who had a theory that soma was a certain mushroom. So I was prepared to take that mythology a little more literally than most Westerners, as signifying something more literal on a spiritual level.' Quoted in Suranjan Ganguly, 'Allen Ginsberg in India,' *Ariel a Review of International English Literature* 24, no. 4 (October 1993): p. 24.

5   See his poem 'On discovering that Soma is a mushroom' in this volume.

6   Frits Staal (1930–2012). Professor of Philosophy and South Asian Studies at University of California, Berkeley. He specialized in Indian logic, linguistics and Vedic studies.

7   A.K. Ramanujan lecture notes, 1979–80. Quoted in Krishna Ramanujan and Guillermo Rodríguez (eds.), *Journeys: A Poet's Diary* (Gurgaon: Penguin Random House, 2019), pp. 243–44.

8   Arthur Antony McDonnell, trans. 'Rig Veda 10.125', *Vedic Mythology* (Strassburg: K. J. Trübner, 1897), p. 109, quoted in AKR's lecture notes, A.K. Ramanujan Papers, Hanna Holborn Gray Special Collections Research Center, University of Chicago Library.

9   The full manuscript of the 'Mescalin Notes' was first published in *Journeys*, pp. 143–69.

10   See below the interviews conducted in 1980, 1981 and 1982.

11   Bruce King, *Modern Indian Poetry in English* (London: Oxford University Press, 1987), pp. 30–45.

12   Though we have no publication of new original poetry in English by AKR in the 1970s after *Relations*, it was certainly a prolific decade for him. Apart from the translation volumes cited, Oxford brought out *Selected Poems* in 1976. The Kannada poetry collection *Mattu Itara Padyagalu* (*And Other Poems*) was published in 1977 in Dharwad by Manohara Grantha Mala. And *Mathobana Atmacaritre* (*Someone Else's Autobiography*), his Kannada novella, in 1978 by the same publisher.

13   The 1970s saw the rise of popular cult figures such as Maharishi Mahesh Yogi and Rajneesh (Osho), who made a great impact on prominent Western musicians, artists and writers, and influenced the global perception of Indian spirituality.

14   A.K. Ramanujan, *Relations* (London and New York: Oxford University Press, 1971), p. 57.

15   See also the essay 'Classics Lost and Found' on Tamil Sangam poetry, in which AKR inserts his own poem 'Prayer to Lord Murugan' as an example of a counter-text to the classical Tamil tradition. Ramanujan, Classics Lost and Found', first published in Carla Borden, ed., *Contemporary India: Essays on the Uses of Tradition* (London: Oxford University Press, 1989), pp. 131–46.

16   For a wider analysis of the import of this episode in AKR's aesthetics see Guillermo Rodríguez, *When Mirrors are Windows. A View of A.K. Ramanujan's Poetics* (New Delhi: Oxford University Press, 2016), pp. 129–30, 135–37.

17   Published in *Journeys*.

18   The translations of this tenth century Tamil saint were published in 1981. A.K. Ramanujan, trans., *Hymns for the Drowning: Poems for Visnu by Nammāḻvār* (Princeton: Princeton University Press, 1981).

19   A.K. Ramanujan, 'Men, Women and Saints', lecture delivered
     at the Center for World Religions, Harvard University
     (1976); incorporated in 'On Women Saints' (1982) and
     'Men, Women and Saints', in Vinay Dharwadker, ed., *The
     Collected Essays of A.K. Ramanujan* (New Delhi: Oxford
     University Press, 1999), pp. 270–78, 279–94.

20   Carlos Castaneda was a notorious American writer who
     popularized shamanistic rituals and the peyote quest through
     his works. His books *The Teachings of Don Juan. A Yaqui
     Way of Knowledge* (Los Angeles: Harvard University Press,
     1968), *A Separate Reality* (New York: Simon & Schuster,
     1971) and *Journey to Ixtlan. The Lessons of Don Juan* (New
     York: Simon & Schuster, 1972) sold millions of copies. The
     poem 'Soma: he looks at autumn leaves' by AKR in this
     volume mentions 'journey to Xtlan'.

21   See above on Ginsberg and soma.

22   A.K. Ramanujan, trans., *Speaking of Siva* (New York:
     Penguin Books, 1973) p. 35.

23   A.K. Ramanujan, Diary, 30 October 1976. See *When Mirrors
     Are Windows*, p. 250, and *Journeys*, p. 203.

24   Ramanujan quoted in A.S. Murali Venkatesh, 'A Poet and
     His Perceptions', *Deccan Herald*, August 17, 1980, Bangalore
     edition.

25   See Chirantan Kulshrestha, 'A.K. Ramanujan: A Profile',
     Journal of South Asian Literature, vol. 16, no. 2 (Summer–
     Fall 1981), pp. 181–84.

26   See the revised edition of the 1982 interview conducted by
     K. Ayyappa Paniker in this book. It was first published in
     2002. Guillermo Rodríguez, ed., 'Afterwords: Ayyappa
     Paniker in Conversation with A.K. Ramanujan (Chicago,
     1982)'. *Journal of Literature and Aesthetics* 2.1 (Jan–June
     2002): pp. 139–50.

27   For a detailed study on AKR's 'Inner Aesthetics' see *When
     Mirrors Are Windows*, pp. 110–64.

28   Doniger, *The Rig Veda: An Anthology of One Hundred and Eight Hymns.*

29   Ramanujan, *Mathobana Atmacaritre*, p. 222.

30   *Journeys*, pp. 176, 180.

31   *Second Sight*, pp. 63–65.

32   *Journeys*, p. 178.

33   Published in *Journeys*, pp. 227–29.

34   AKR's first poetry collections in English, as mentioned above, were *The Striders* (1966) and *Relations* (1971), both published by Oxford University Press in London.

35   See, for instance, 'A Poem on Particulars', in *The Striders*, pp. 51–52.

36   This line, as A.K. Mehrotra points out in the Foreword of this book, echoes John Donne. See also AKR's opening early poem 'The Striders', below.

37   See also the poem 'Soma', below.

38   And on decreasing and increasing, or 'growing on the line / between left and right', as the Soma poem goes, there is this passage in Alice's Adventures in Wonderland, where the caterpillar and Alice converse about the effect of eating the mushroom: '"One side will make you grow taller, and the other side will make you grow shorter." "One side of what? The other side of what?" thought Alice to herself. "Of the mushroom," said the Caterpillar . . .' Lewis Carroll, *Alice's Adventures in Wonderland* (London: Macmillan and Co., 1866), p. 68.

        Critics and readers, notably during the counterculture years from the 1960s to 1980s, were quick to point out the psychedelic nature of this novel. Whether this apparently innocent text was the consequence of a drug-infused experience is still a matter of controversy.

39   'Jazz Poem for Soma' was published in *Journeys*, pp. 229–30. The last phrase is in italics, though the original source is a handwritten manuscript that does not use italics.

40 See the section on 'Mutual Cannibalism' in the Afterword to *Hymns for the Drowning*, pp. 150–51.
41 From Nammāḻvār's *Tiruvāymoḻi*, 10.7.1
42 The handwritten note scribbled next to the draft 'Jazz Poem for Soma' has been published in *When Mirrors Are Windows*, p. 439.
43 See the full poem published in this volume.
44 AKR quoted in Venkatesh, 'A Poet and His Perceptions'.
45 For AKR's critical 'model' for Indian literature see also *When Mirrors Are Windows*, pp. 32–43.
46 See A.K. Ramanujan, *Poems of Love and War: From the Eight Anthologies and the Ten Long Poems of Classical Tamil* (New York: Columbia University Press, 1985).
47 See AKR's comments in an earlier interview conducted by Chirantan Kulshrestha in 1970. Daniels–Ramanujan, Molly, and Keith Harisson, eds., 'Chirantan Kulshrestha and AKR', interview conducted at the University of Chicago in 1970, in *Uncollected Poems and Prose: A.K. Ramanujan* (London and New Delhi: Oxford University Press, 2001), p. 46.
48 *Journeys*, p. 292
49 See 'Elements of Composition', *Second Sight*, p. 11. For the transition from 'Composition' to *Second Sight* see 'The Making of a 'Composition': A.K. Ramanujan's *Second Sight*', *When Mirrors Are Windows* pp. 434–53.
50 This is the last line of a famous medieval Kannada bhakti poem by Basavanna translated by AKR. See *Speaking of Siva*, p. 88.
51 Which reminds me of the mushroom connection, the fly agaric. The mushroom–insect relationship is one of fatal attraction: *Amanita muscaria* means 'fly poison' and was used as an insecticide. Some theories speculate that insects intentionally seek out the plant because of its intoxicating or medicinal qualities.
52 The 'I/eye' pun is from Ezra Pound, who 'walked eye-deep in hell' in 'Hugh Selwyn Mauberly'.

53 'The Striders', *The Striders*, 1. A first draft of this poem dated 26 March 1960 in the AKR Papers is titled 'Fear'. See *When Mirrors Are Windows* p. 237.

The Post-Vedic History of the Soma Plant

1   Monier-Williams' dictionary gives 'distilled liquor' as a primary meaning of súrā, but evidence is strong that the distilling process was not known in India until a much later era.

2   Śatapatha Brāhmaṇa, Chowkhamba edition, 5.I.2.10.

3   *Taittirīya Brāhmaṇa*, Ānandāśrama edition, 1.3.3.2.

4   Śatapatha Brāhmaṇa, 4.5.10.2-6.

5   *Tāṇḍya Brāhmaṇa*, Bibliotheca Indica edition, 9.5.1.

6   *Tāṇḍya Brāhmaṇa*, 9.5.3.

7   *Aitareya Brāhmaṇa*, Haug edition, 7.5.30.

8   *Kātyāyna Śrautasūtra*, Albrecht Weber, ed., Berlin, 1859, verse 7.8.13.

9   Śatapatha Brāhmaṇa, 5.3.3.4.

10   Cf. Hemacandra, *Abhidhānacintāmaṇi*, ed. Böhtlingk and Roth, St. Petersburg, 1849, 1191-1192.

11   Cf. *Kauṣītaki Brāhmaṇa*, Ānandāśrama edition, 2.2. and *Śatapatha Brāhmaṇa*, 6.6.3.7.

12   H.H. Wilson, *Sanskrit Dictionary*, 1832, defines *phālguna* as 'a red plant, *Arjutuna pentaptera*.'

13   Rudolph von Roth, in his 1881 article in the *Zeitschrift der Deutschen Morgenländischen Gesellschaft*, 'Über den Soma', identified the red *dúrvā* grass with the *Cynodon dactylon* that the Indians used, according to Roxburgh, to make a drink, 'a very cheap kind of Soma' (*eine sehr billige Soma*), as Roth remarked.

14   *Taittirīya Samhitā*, Keith edition, 6.1.6; Śatapatha Brāhmaṇa, 3.3.1.15.

15   *Amarakośa*, Kielhorn edition, Bombay, 2.4.82-3 and 2.4.95.

16 *Ibid.*, 2.10.39. Amara gives as synonyms for *súrā* the terms *varuṇātmayā*, *halipriyā*, and *pariśrut*; the latter may refer to an intoxicating liquor made from herbs or to the Soma of the Vedas (ṚgVeda IX I[6], and *Śatapatha Brāhmaṇa* 12.7.1.7).

17 *Medinīkośa*, Nathalal Laxmichand edition, 36.

18 Yāska's *Nighaṇṭu and Nirukta*, Laksman Sarup, ed., University of the Punjab, 1927; 11.2.2. and 5.17. *prīṇāti nacamanena* is given as the etymology for *nicumpana*.

19 Commentary on ṚgVeda III 48[2]. Max Müller edition.

20 Śabarasvāmi, commentary on the *Pūrva Mimāṃsa Sūtra*, Gaekwad edition, 2.2.17. Soma is called *latā kṣīriṇī*.

21 This ascription to Soma, of a 'milky' quality, was probably based on the Vedic statements that Soma was mixed with milk, or that Soma itself became white when mixed with milk, or that the juice of Soma was 'milk' in the metaphorical sense of the supreme liquid, or the liquid pressed out of a swollen container; for it must be noted that nowhere in the Vedas is the raw Soma juice itself described as white or milky, but always as yellow or brown or red or golden.

22 *Dhanvantarīyanighaṇṭu*, Ānandāśrama Series no. 33, Poona, 1896; verse 4.4.

23 *Rājanighaṇṭu*, Ānandāśrama Series no. 33; verses 3.29-3.30. The pertinent terms are: *mahāgulmā dhanurvallī*; *katuś śitā madhurā*; *pittadāhakṛt* (or alternate reading: *pittadāhanut*); *tṛsnāviśoṣaśamanī* (alternate reading: *kṛṣṇā viśoṣaśamanī*); and *pāvanī* (or *pācani*).

24 *Suśrutasaṃhitā*, Education Press, Calcutta, 1834, chap. 29. I have been unable to find the quotation in other editions of this work, but it is quoted in full in the *Śabdakalpadruma* (vol. v, p. 417), Calcutta, 1814, which attributes it to the *Suśruta*. It will be noted that several of the Suśruta's 'varieties' of Soma refer to substitutes mentioned in the Brāhmaṇas.

25 This lunar connection is an extrapolation of the mythological association of Soma with the moon in the Vedas, and it accounts

for the name 'moon-plant' given to Soma by the Bengalis of
the last century. Yet Edward Balfour, in his *Cyclopædia of
India*, published in London in 1885, maintained that the
Soma plant itself derived its name from the Sanskrit word for
moon, *soma*, because 'it was gathered by moonlight.'

26   Cited by F. Max Müller in 'Die Todtenbestattung bei den
Brahmanen', *Zeitschrift der Deutschen Morgenländischen
Gesellschaft*, no. 39. 1855. pp. XLII–XLIII. The text reads:

> śyāmalā 'mlā ca niṣpatrā   kṣīriṇī tvaci māṃsalā
> śleṣmalā vamanī vallī   somākhyā chāgabhojanam

27   *Yašt* fragment 21.9. This and the following are from the
edition of James Darmesteter and L. H. Mills, *Sacred Books
of the East*, Volumes 4, 23, and 31.

28   *Ashi Yašt*, 2.5, and *Yasna*, 10.8.

29   *Sirozah*, 2.30.

30   *Ashi Yašt*, 6.37, Gos *Yašt*, 4.17, and *Mihir Yašt*, 23.88.

31   *Yasna*, 10.3

32   *Yasna*, 10.2.

33   *Yasna*, 10.4.

34   *Yasna*, 10.5; *vide supra*, pp. 19–21.

35   *Yasna*, 10.13.

36   *Yasna*, 9.16.

37   Henrik Samnel Nyberg: *Die Religionen des Alten Irans*,
Leipzig, 1938, pp. 188, 244, and 288.

38   Megasthenes, *Indika*, translated by J. W. McCrindle,
Calcutta, 1887 (Schwanbeck edition, Bonn, 1846), fragment
27, page 69. Quoted by Strabo, 15.1.53–56.

39   Plutarch: *De Iside et Osire*, Squire edition, 1744, p. 117; μζ
[mz].

40   *Vide infra; p. 108.

41   Emile Benveniste, *The Persian Religion: According to the
Chief Greek Texts. 1909*, p. 74. The *amomum* is thought to be
the Indian spice plant, *Nepaul cardamom*. It is mentioned in

Aristophanes' *The Frogs,* 110, and in Theophrastes' *Historia Plantarum,* 9.7.2, where it is said to come from India as cardamom comes from Persia.

42 A.H. Anquetil–Duperron, *Zend-Avesta, traduit par Anquetil du Perron,* Paris, 1771, vol. II, p. 535.

43 Charles Wilkins, *The Bhāgvāt Geeta,* Serampore, 1784, p. 80, note 42.

44 Sir William Jones, *Institutes of Hindu Law, or, the Ordinances of Manu,* Calcutta, 1794, verse 3.158.

45 H.T. Colebrooke, *Cosha or Dictionary of the Sanscrit Language, by Amaru Sinha, with an English Interpretation and Annotations* by *H.T. Colebrooke, Esq.,* Serampore, 1808, p. 102, note on verse 4.3.14. It should be added that Amara distinguished this plant from the *somavallī* for which Colebrooke gives no botanical name.

46 Colebrooke, *op. cit.,* p. 10.

47 William Carey, *Hortus Bengalensis, A Catalogue of the Plants Described* by *Dr. Roxburgh in his Manuscript Flora Indica,* Calcutta, 1814, pp. 20 and 32.

48 *Ibid.,* p. xi.

49 Horace Hayman Wilson, *Sanskrit Dictionary,* Calcutta, 1819 and 1832. In identifying *somavallī* with *Menispermum glabrum,* Wilson was misled by Colebrooke, whose Amara Simha he cites for this reference; Colebrooke, though giving no definition of *somavallī,* had given *Menispermum glabrum* (= *Tinospora cordifolia*) for the plant *guḍucī (guricha* in Colebrooke's note) which appeals in juxtaposition with *somavallī* in the *Amarakosa.*

50 William Roxburgh, *Flora Indica,* Serampore, 1832, vol. II. p. 33.

51 *Ibid.,* vol. III, p. 406.

52 George Watt, *Dictionary of the Economic Products of India,* Calcutta, 1890, cites these examples in his article on 'Ephedra.' *Vide infra,* p. 121.

53 Henry Piddington, *An English Index to the Plants of India,* Calcutta, 1832, pp. 9 and 79.

54 John Stevenson, *Sanhitā of the Sāma Veda,* London, 1842, p. iv

55 Eugène Burnouf, 'Études sur la langue et sur les textes zends. IV: Le Dieu Homa,' in *Journal Asiatique,* 8th Series, no. 4, December, 1844, p. 468.

56 J.O. Voigt, *Hortus Suburbanus Calcuttensis, A Catalogue of the Plants in the Honourable East India Company Botanical Garden,* Calcutta, 1845, pp. 405 and 542.

57 *Ibid.,* p. 539.

58 Friedrich Windischmann, 'Über den Somakultus der Arier', *Abhandlungen der Königlichen Baierischen Akadamie der Wissenschaften,* Munich, 1846, pp. 127–42.

59 Christian Lassen, *Indische Altertumskunde,* Bonn 1847, vol. 1, p. 281.

60 William Dwight Whitney, 'On the main results of Vedic researches in Germany', *Journal of the American Oriental Society,* no. 3 (1853): p. 299.

61 Otto Böhtlingk and Rudolph von Roth, *Sanskritwörterbuch nebst allen Nachträgen,* St. Petersburg, 1855–75.

62 *Vide supra,* p. 100.

63 F. Max Müller, 'Die Todtenbestattung bei den Brahmanen,' *Zeitschrift der Deutschen Morgenländischen Gesellschaft,* no. 39, 1855, p. xlii ff.

64 Major Heber Drury, *Useful Plants of India,* Madras, 1858, p. 385.

65 Walter Elliot, *Flora Andhrica, A Vernacular and Botanical List of Plants Commonly Met with in the Telegu District,* Madras, 1859, p. 169.

66 Martin Haug, *Essays on the Religion of the Parsees,* 1861; pp. 219–222, and *Aitareya Brāhmaṇa,* Bombay, 1863, vol. II, p. 489.

67 Sir George Christopher Birdwood, *Catalogue of the Vegetable Productions of the Presidency of Bombay,* Bombay, 1865, p. 53.

68 *Ibid.,* p. 209.

69 J. Forbes Watson, *Index to Native and Scientific Names of Indian and Other Economic Plants and Products,* London, 1866, p. 530.

70 Paul Anton de Lagarde, *Gesammelte Abhandlungen,* Leipzig, 1866, p. 174.

71 *Odyssey,* x, pp. 304–05.

72 Jacob Ludwig Grimm, *Deutsche Mythologie,* Göttingen, 1835, p. 962, had mentioned that rue was used in sacrifices to the devil.

73 Lagarde, *op. cit.,* p. 175.

74 The term *sahásrapājas,* occurring only twice in the ṚgVeda (IX 13³ and IX 42³), is generally translated as 'possessing a thousand forms,' or 'colours', or 'rays'.

75 John Garrett, *Classical Dictionary of India,* Madras, 1871, p. 594.

76 Joseph Dalton Hooker, *Curtis's Botanical Magazine,* London, 1872, tab. 6002.

77 Major Heber Drury, *Useful Plants of India* (2nd edition), London, 1873

78 Hermann Grassmann, *Wörterbuch zum Rig Veda,* Leipzig, 1873.

79 Rajendra Lala Mitra, 'Spirituous Drinks in Ancient India', *Journal of the Royal Asiatic Society of Bengal,* 1873, p. 2.

80 *Ibid.,* p. 21.

81 Arthur Coke Burnell, *Elements of South Indian Palæography,* Mangalore, 1874, p. I.

82 Martin Haug, in a review of Grassmann's *Wörterbuch; Göttingische Gelehrte Anzeigen,* 1875, pp. 584–95.

83 Friedrich Spiegel, *Eranische Alterthumskunde, Leipzig,* 1878, vol. III, p. 572.

84 Abel Bergaigne, *La Religion Védique,* Paris, 1878, vol. 1, pp. ix and 148.

85 Heinrich Zimmer, *Altindisches Leben,* Berlin, 1879, p. 275.

86 Rajendra Lala Mitra, *Indo–Aryans*, London, 1881, pp. 390–419.

87 Kenneth Somerled Macdonald, *The Vedic Religion*, London, 1881, p. 66.

88 Rudolph von Roth, 'Über den Soma', *Zeitschrift der Deutschen Morgenländischen Gesellschaft*, no. 35, 1881, pp, 680–92.

89 Edward William West, *Pahlavi Texts, Sacred Books of the East*, vol. 18, 1882, p. 164.

90 Angelo de Gubernatis, *La Mythologie des Plantes*, Paris, 1882, vol. II, pp. 350–69.

91 Sir Monier Monier–Williams, *Religious Thought and Life in India*, London, 1883. pp. 12–13.

92 D.N. Ovsianiko–Kulikovskij: Zapiski *Imperatorskogo Novorasükogo Universiteta*, vol. 39, Odessa, 1884. Chast' 1: *Kul't bozhestva Soma v Drevnei Indii v epokhu* Ved. [Part I: The Cult of the Deity 'Soma' in Ancient India in the Vedic Epoch] I am indebted to D.M. O'Flaherty for the translation.

93 *Ibid.*, p. 7.

94 *Ibid.*, p. 8

95 *Idem.* This peculiar notion appeals only one year later in the Cyclopædia of Edward Balfour (vide *supra*, p. 99), but it is most unlikely that he knew Ovsianiko-Kurlikovskij's work.

96 *Ibid.*, p. 9.

97 Ovsianiko–Kulikovskij, *op. cit*, p. 12.

98 Rudolph von Roth, 'Wo wächst der Soma?', *Zeitschrift der Deutschen Morgenländischen Gesellschaft*, no. 38, 1884. pp. 134–39.

99 The πήγανον [píganon] and harmal to which Lagarde had referred.

100 That the Aryans knew of such a fruit and of an alcoholic drink made from it is established by Pāṇini's reference to the sweet grape juice of Kāpiśī, north of Kabul (Pāṇini 4.2.99).

101 *Vide supra*, pp. 100 and 107.

102 Here he refers to de Gubernatis II, 352; *vide supra*, p. 112.

103 This is not true. *Phala*, 'fruit,' recurs in the ṚgVeda, referring to the fruit of a plant (not Soma) rather than to the stem. Cf. ṚgVeda III 45[4], IV 57[6], x 71[5], x 97[15] and x 146[5].

104 Surgeon General Edward Balfour, *The Cyclopædia of India and of Eastern and Southern Asia, Commercial. Industrial, and Scientific; Products of the Mineral, Vegetable, and Animal Kingdoms, Useful Arts and Manufactures* (3rd edition), London, 1885, vol. III, p. 703.

105 Julius Eggeling, *Śatapathā Brāhmaṇa, Sacred Books of the East*, vol. II (1885), p. xxiv ff.

106 I.E. Aitchison, *The Botany of the Afghan Delimitation Commission,* Transactions of the Linnæan Society, London, 1887, p. 112.

107 Max Müller, *Collected Works,* London, 1888, vol. x, pp. 222–42.

108 George Watt, 'Ephedra', *Dictionary of the Economic Products of India,* Calcutta, 1890.

109 Adalbert Kuhn, *Mythologische Studien,* Gütersloh, 1886, vol. I, p. 106.

110 John Firminger Duthie, *The Fodder Grasses of North India,* Roorkee,1888, p. 14.

111 *Vide supra,* pp. 59–60.

112 James Darmesteter, *Avesta,* translation into French, Paris, 1890–1892; introduction, p. lxv. He gives a picture of the plant as well (*vide* fig. 4).

113 J. Börnmuller, 'Reisebriefe aus Persien', in *Mitteilungen des Thüringischen Botanischen Verlags,* 1893, p. 42.

114 Alfred Hillebrandt, *Vedische Mythologie,* Breslau, 1891, vol. 1, pp. 1–18.

115 This word, however, occurs only once in the ṚgVeda (III 53[14]) and its meaning is uncertain; Grassmann thinks that it may refer to the name of a sage.

116 Hermann Oldenberg, *Die Religion des Veda,* Berlin, 1894. p. 366 ff.

117 Edmund Hardy, *Die Vedische-Brahmanische Periode,* Münster, 1893, pp. 152–53.

118 Zenalde A. Ragozin, *Vedic India,* London, 1895, p. 171; W. Caland, *Altindische Zauberritual,* Amsterdam, 1900, p. 188.

119 P. Regnaud, 'Remarques sur le IXème Maṇḍala du ṚgVeda', *Revue de l'Histoire Religieuse, XLIII,* 1902, pp. 308–13.

120 Rustomjee Naserwanyil Khory, *Materia Medica of India and their Therapeutics,* Bombay, 1903.

121 W.W. Wilson, 'The Soma offering in a fragment of Alkman,' *American Journal of Philology,* no. 30, 1906, pp. 188–95. Roth in his 1884 essay had suggested that Soma in India had occupied a sacred position similar to that held by the now extinct σιλφιον [silfion] plant of Ancient Greece, but he had not considered the two plants identical.

122 W. Caland and Victor Henry, *L'Agniṣṭoma,* Paris, 1906–7. p. 471.

123 Victor Henry, *Soma et Haoma,* Paris, 1907, p. 52.

124 Maurice Bloomfield, *The Religion of the Veda,* New York, 1908, p. 145.

125 Arthur Anthony Macdonell and Arthur Berriedale Keith, *Vedic Index,* London, 1912, vol. II, p. 475.

126 Hermann Brunnhofer, *Arische Urzeit,* Bern, 1910, p. 297.

127 *Ibid.,* p. 300. The quotation from Pliny (*Historia Naturatis* 27.28.11) merely says that of several plants bearing the name of αμβροσία [amvrosía], one has leaves around the bottom of the stem resembling those of rue *(foliis rutæ circa imum caulem).* Elsewhere (*Historia Naturalis* 14–40), Pliny speaks of αμβροσία as a kind of grape.

128 C. Hartwich, *Die menschlichen Genussmittel,* Leipzig, 1911, p. 806 ff.

129 Hartwich, *op. cit.,* p. 809.

130 *Ibid.,* p. 808.

131 *Indrasurā* (also known as Indrasurasa and Indrasurisa) is mentioned in the *Amarakośa,* the *Suśruta Saṃhitā,* and the *Śabdakalpadruma,* but is nowhere associated with Soma.

132 Indrāśana as a name for hemp (perhaps by confusion with *Indra-śaṇa*, which would mean the hemp of Indra) is mentioned in the *Śabdamālā* (quoted in the *Śabdakalpadruma*) and appears in its prākrit form - *Indrāsana-* in *Dhūrtasamāgama* 90.8.

133 A. B. Keith: The *Taittirīya Saṃhitā*, Harvard Oriental Series, Volumes 18 and 19, 1914, introduction and p. 119.

134 L.H. Mills, 'The Avestic H(a)oma and the Vedic Soma', *Asiatic Review*, no. 8, 1916, p. 315.

135 Vincent Smith, *Oxford History of India*, 1919, p. 33.

136 E.W. Hopkins: 'Soma,' in Hastings' *Encyclopædia of Religion and Ethics*, vol. II, Edinburgh, 1910, p. 685.

137 Chapman Cohen, *Religion and Sex*, Edinburgh, 1919, p. 57.

138 E.B. Havell, 'What is Soma?', in the *Journal of the Royal Asiatic Society*, 1920, p. 349 ff.

139 ṚgVeda IX 113.

140 Braja Lal Mukherjee, 'The Soma Plant', *Journal* of the *Royal Asiatic Society*, 1921, p. 241.

141 This is untrue. *Vide supra*, p. 43.

142 This verse does not refer to Soma at all, but verses 3.4.3.13 and 4.2.5.15 of the Mādhyandina recension of the Śatapatha Brāhmaṇa speak of a plant called *uśānā*, from which Soma is made.

143 The Durgā celebration, the use of *bhang* and the tradition that Śiva uses *bhang*, are all late characteristics of Bengal Śaivism.

144 Braja Lal Mukherjee, *The Soma Plant*, Calcutta. 1922.

145 L.D. Barnett, Review in *Journal of the Royal Asiatic* Society, 1923, p. 437.

146 Sir Charles Eliot, *Hinduism and Buddhism*, London, 1921, vol. 1, p. 69.

147 N.B. Pavgee, *The Indigenous Far-Famed Soma and the Aryan Autochthones in India*, Poona, 1921, and 'Soma juice is not liquor.' Third Oriental Conference, 1924, pp. 70–79.

148 Jakob Wilhelm Hauer, *Die Anfänge der Yogapraxis im Alten Indien*, Berlin, 1922, p.137.

149 *Ibid.*, p. 57, 59, 61.

150 Hauer, *op. cit.*, p. 62.

151 Gilbert Slater, *The Dravidian Element in Indian Culture*, London, 1924. p. 78.

152 Georges Dumézil, 'Le Festin d'Immortalité', *Annales du Musée Guimet*, no. 34, 1924, p. 279.

153 Śatapatha Brāhmaṇa, 3.6.1.8-9.

154 Dumézil, *op. cit*, p. 285.

155 Louis Lewin, *Phantastica: die betäubenden und erregenden Genussmittel*, Leipzig, 1924; published in London, 1931, as *Phantastica: Narcotic and Stimulating Drugs*, from which I cite the above information, p. 161, note.

156 *Ibid.*, p. 117.

157 L.L. Uhl, '*A contribution towards the identification of the Soma plant of Vedic times,*' in *Journal of the American Oriental Society*, no. 45, 1915, p. 351.

158 A.B. Keith, *Religion and Philosophy of the Vedas and Upanishads*, Harvard Oriental Series, Volumes 31–32, 1925, pp. 173, 283–4, 482.

159 *Ibid.*, p. 402.

160 Roth and Whitney, eds., *Atharvaveda*, Berlin, 1855, IV.5.

161 Keith, *op. cit.*, p. 172.

162 G. Jouveau–Dubreuil, 'Soma', in the *Indian Antiquary*, trans., Sir R. Temple, 1916, no. 55, p. 176.

163 Otto Schrader and A. Nehring, *Reallexikon der Indogermanischen Altertumskunde*, Berlin, 1929, vol. II, p. 139.

164 P.V. Kane, *History of Dharmaśāstra, 1930–62*, vol. II, part 2, chap. 33, pp. 1202–03.

165 Sir Aurel Stein, 'On the Ephedra, the Hum Plant, and the Soma,' *Bulletin of the London School of Oriental Studies*, 6/2, 1931, p. 501 ff.

166 Sir Aurel noted that Albert Regel had suggested rhubarb in 1884. *Vide supra*, p. 114.

167 Stein *op. cit.*, p. 513.

168 Paul Lindner, 'Das Geheimnis um Soma,' *Forschungen und Fortschritte*, no. 5, 1933, p. 65.

169 E. Hubers, 'Schilderungen der Bierbereitung im fernen Osten', in *Mitteilungen der Gesellschaft für Bibliographie und Geschichte des Brauwesens.* Lindner also cited J. Arnolds' *Origin and History of Beer and Brewing.*

170 *'Unvermindertes Wohlbefinden und fast geruchlose Exkremente.'*

171 Philippe de Félice, *Poisons Sacrés, Ivresses Divines: Essai sur quelques formes inférieures de la mystique,* Paris, 1936, pp. 265–66.

172 The Indo–Aryans, spreading out east and south from the Indus Valley, were finding themselves increasingly remote from the Hindu Kush and the Himalayas.

173 Śatapatha Brāhmaṇa 1.6.3.1-7.

174 L. van Itallie, *'Soma-Haoma,* de heilige plant der Indiërs en der Perzen,' *Natuurwetenschappelijk tijdschrift,* no. 19 (1937), pp. 1 and 9–11.

175 Johannes Hertel, 'Das Indogermanische Neujahrsopfer im Veda', in *Mitteilungen der Sächsischen Akademie der Wissenschaften,* vol. 90, 1938, p. 83.

176 Henrik Samnel Nyberg, *Die Religionen des Alten Irans,* Leipzig, 1938, pp. 177,190, 390 and 341. He cites several Avestan references to hemp, among them *Yašt* 13.124, *Vendidad* 15.14, *Vendidad* 19.20,. *Yasna* 44–20, and *Vendidad* 19–41. W.B. Henning rebutted this argument in his *Zoroaster: Politician or Witch-Doctors,* Oxford, 1951; he considered Nyberg's theory one to be rejected 'without further consideration . . . if one reflects on the effects of hemp, the physical, mental and moral deterioration it brings,' and he maintained that the Avestan citations, 'if correctly interpreted, can at the most serve to show that they cultivated hemp, possibly for the purpose for which hemp is cultivated all the world over—i.e., to obtain its fibre.'

177 Nyberg, *op.* cit., p. 288.

178 ṚgVeda IX 61.[13] *Bhaṅgá* here seems to be an epithet meaning 'intoxicating' (from *bhañj,* to break, *i.e.,* to disrupt the senses), but the reading occurs only once and is uncertain.

Macdonell suggests that the word *bhangá* first applied to Soma, meaning 'intoxicating,' and then 'came to designate hemp' (*Vedic Index,* vol. II, p. 93). Otto Schrader suggests that *bhang* 'was originally prized for the intoxicating effects of its decoctions' *(Prehistoric Antiquities of the Aryan Peoples,* translated from the German and published in London, 1890, p. 299), but after the one questionable Vedic occurrence, *bhanga* appears in classical Sanskrit several time only to designate the plant, with no reference to any narcotic effects. The eighth century AD. *Śārngadhara Saṃhitā* (Bombay, 1888; 1–4.19) is the first extant source that considers *bhangā* a drug; it likens it to 'the saliva of a snake,' *i.e.,* opium *(phenam cāhisamudbhavam)* and the commentator adds that the effect is like that of inebriating liquor *(madyaviṣayavat).* The *Bhāvaprakāśa* (Chowkhamba edition, 1.1) refers to *bhangā* (*mātulāni*) as intoxicating and causing hallucination (*moha*) and slow speech *(mandavāk),* and the *Dhanvantarīya-nighaṇṭu* describes *bhangā* as intoxicating, bitter, stimulating talk, inducing sleep and producing hallucinations.

179 Joges Candra Roy, 'The Soma Plant', *Indian Historical Quarterly,* no. 15, June 1939, pp. 197–207.

180 Delli Roman Regni, 'The control of liquor in Ancient India', *New Review,* Calcutta, November 1940, p. 382.

181 C. Kunham Raja, 'Was Soma an intoxicating drink of the People?', *Adyar Library Bulletin,* no. 10, 1946, pp. 90–105.

182 Ernst Herzfeld, *Zoroaster and his World,* Princeton, 1947, vol. II, p. 543 ff.

183 Bracketed material appears elsewhere in Herzfeld.

184 The first certain European reference to the use of hemp as a drug in India is in Garcia d'Orta's record of a conversation with the Sultan Badar in Goa in 1563. The Sultan confessed that whenever in the night he had a desire to visit Portugal, Turkey and Arabia, 'all he had to do was to eat a little *bangue* . . .' In 1676, Henrich van Rheede (van Draakenstein), the governor of Malabar, published his *Hortus Indicus*

Malabaricus in Amsterdam (written in Latin and Dutch), in which he called attention to a plant named *bangi* that was smoked like tobacco and caused inebriation (vol. 10, p. 67). George Everhard Rumph in 1755 described at length, in Latin, the effect of the *Cannabis sativa* (also known as *ginji*) upon the natives, likening the plant to the Homeric νηπενθές [nipenthés]: ' . . . For the inhabitants of these regions, not content with the natural virtue of wine, which, however, they do not possess in great quantity, or with the other types of wine tree of that place, on the ground that in their opinion it elates one for a short time only, have devised from this plant such things as are able at a moment to remove anxieties of the heart, grief, or fear of dangers; yet this cannot be, except by a violent commotion of the senses and clouding of the intellect, which they themselves call drunkenness but we call inanity, which is usually followed by mania or a stupid condition.' (Rumphius, *Herbarium Amboinense,* Amsterdam, (1755), vol. 5, p. 208). By 1868, *bhang* was so well known that Lord Neaves honored it with this bit of doggerel:

> The hemp—with which we used to hang
> Our prison pets, yon felon gang—
> In Eastern climes produces Bang,
> Esteemed a drug divine.

185 R.N. Chopra, S.C. Nayar, L.C. Chopra, *Glossary of Indian Medicinal Plants,* 1956.

186 R. N. Chopra et al.: *Poisonous Plants of India,* 1949, Vol. I, p. 683.

187 R.N. Chopra, S. Krishna and T.P. Ghose, 'Indian Ephedras, their Chemistry and Pharmacology,' *Indian Journal of Medical Research,* no. 19, 1931–32, pp. 177–219; and *cf.* S. Krishna and T.P. Ghose, 'Indian Ephedras and their Extraction,' *Journal of the Indian Society of Chemistry,* no. 48, 1929, p. 67.

188 Karl Geldner, *Der Rig-Veda,* published in Harvard Oriental Series, Volumes 33–35, 1951, vol. III, p. 2. Part 1 of an

earlier version of Geldner's translation had been published in Leipzig in 1923, but Geldner died before the completion of Part III (which included the Soma hymns).

189 Chinnaswami Sastri, 'Sama-svarūpavimarśa', in *Our Heritage,* no. I, Calcutta, 1953, pp. 80–86.

190 Reinhold F.G. Müller, 'Soma in der Altindischen Heilkunde', *Asiatica, Festschrift für Friedrich Weller,* Leipzig, 1954, p. 428–41.

191 Patañjali (*Yogasūtram,* Kāśī Sanskrit Series, no. 85, Benares, 1931; verse 4-1) states that *auṣadhi* (herbs) and *samādhi* (meditation) are methods of obtaining *siddhi* (perfection through yoga).

192 Mircea Eliade, *Le Yoga, Immortalité et Liberté,* Paris, 1954, republished by Bollingen, 1958, in English translation as *Yoga: Immortality and Freedom,* p. 338.

193 A.L. Basham, *The Wonder That Was India,* London, 1954, pp. 235–36.

194 K.M. Nadkarni and A.K. Nadkarni, *Indian Materia Medica,* Bombay, 1954.

195 P.V. Sharma, *Dravya Gun Vigyan,* Benares, 1956.

196 r̥jīṣá (which occurs only once, R̥gVeda 1 32[6]) is thought by some to refer to the part of the Soma stalk left over after the juice has been expressed; Grassmann takes it to mean 'rushing forward freely', and, as it applies to India rather than Soma, this is more likely. *tiróahnya,* 'having lasted through yesterday', is an adjective applied to Soma.

197 V.G. Rahurkar, 'Was Soma a spirituous liquor?', *Oriental Thought,* no. 2, 1955, pp. 131–49.

198 B.H. Kapadia, *A Critical Interpretation and Investigation of Soma,* Mahavidyalaya, Vallabha, 1959. pp. 4 and 35.

199 *atasá* means 'bush, undergrowth, or shrub'; *vána* means 'tree'. Their relationship with Soma in the R̥gVeda is inconclusive.

200 Pentii Aalto, 'Madyam apeyam,' in *Johannes Nobel Commemoration Volume,* Jñānamuktāvalī International Academy of Indian Culture, New Delhi, 1959, pp. 17–37.

201 Dr Karl Hummel, 'Aus welcher Pflanze stellen die arischen Inder den Somatrank her?', *Mitteilungen der Deutschen Pharmazeutischen Gesellschaft und der Pharmazeutischen Gesellschaft der DDR*, Tübingen, April 1959. pp. 57–61.

202 N.A. Qazilbash, 'Ephedra of the Rigveda,' *The Pharmaceutical Journal*, London, November 1960, pp. 497–501.

203 R. Hegnauer, in his *Chemotaxonomie der Pflanzen* (Basel, 1962, vol. I, pp. 451–60), discusses in detail the toxic effects of various Ephedras, identifying several of them with the Soma plant on the basis of Qazilbash's work.

204 G.M. Patil, 'Soma the Vedic Deity', *Oriental Thought*, no. 4. 1960, pp. 69–79.

205 Jan Gonda, *Die Religionen Indiens*, Stuttgart, 1960, vol. I, p. 64.

206 Alain Daniélou, *Le Polythéisme Hindou*, Paris, 1960, p. 111.

207 Alain Daniélou, *L'Érotisme Divinisé*, Paris, 1962, p. 53.

208 Agehananda Bharati (Leopold Fischer), *The Tantric Tradition*, London, 1965, p. 287.

209 *Vide supra*, p. 96. The belief that the Soma was brought from heaven by a falcon appears frequently throughout the ṚgVeda and other Indo–European sources, *cf.* A. Kuhn, *Mythologische Studien, I: Die Herabkunft des Feuers und des Göttertranks*, Gütersloh, 1886. Also cf. ṚgVeda I 80[2], III 43[7] IV 18[13], IV 26[6], V 45[9], IX 68[6], IX 77[2], IX 86[24], X 11[4], X 99[8], X 144[4], etc.

210 Varro B. Tyler, Jr., 'The Physiological Properties and Chemical Constituents of Some Habit-Forming Plants: Soma–Homa, Divine Plant of the Ancient Aryans', *Lloydia*, vol. 29, no. 4, December 1966, p. 284.

211 Ibid., p. 285.

212 ṚgVeda ix 5[10]. *Sahásravalśam,* the adjective in question, modifies *vánaspátim*, which refers to the tree of sacrifice, not to the Soma plant.

213 J.G. Srivastava, 'The Soma Plant', *Quarterly Journal of Crude Drug Research*, no. 6 (1966), 1, p. 811. This seems

to be a translation of the phrase cited above and translated as 'having great clusters' (vide supra, p. 99).

214 Srivastava does not give the Sanskrit for this particular phrase but it may be a translation of amśuman (vide supra, p. 99).

215 Srivastava, op. cit, p. 816.

216 J.P. Kooger, 'Het Raadsel van de Heilige Soma-Plant der Indo–Iraniers', Pharmaceutisch Tijdschrift voor België, 44th year, no. 7, 1967, pp. 137–43

217 R.C. Zaehner, The Dawn and Twilight of Zoroastrianism, London, 1961, p. 88.

218 In this context, it is interesting to note that by 1884 Regel had rejected bhang (Cannabis indica) as a possibility for the Soma plant. Vide supra, p. 114.

219 Aldous Huxley, Island, Penguin ed., 1964, p. 140.

220 An essay published in The Book of Grass, an anthology edited by George Andrews and Simon Vinkenoog, Grove Press Inc., New York, 1967, pp. 192–201. The passage cited is on p. 200.

K. Ayyappa Paniker in conversation with A.K. Ramanujan

1 Guillermo Rodríguez, ed., 'Afterwords: Ayyappa Paniker in Conversation with A.K. Ramanujan (Chicago, 1982)' Journal of Literature and Aesthetics 2.1 (Jan–June 2002): pp. 139–50. In 2009, the then editor of the Sahitya Akademi journal Indian Literature, Kerala poet K. Satchidandan, republished the conversation without crediting the earlier publication and editorial work. See Indian Literature 254 (Nov–Dec 2009): pp. 171–87.

2 John Oliver Perry, 'The Integrity of A.K. Ramanujan's Poetry', Kavya Bharathi, vol. 16 (2004), p. 87.

3 In Indian poetics and linguistics, a measure of the length of a syllable.